Praise for *Sara Triumphant!*

As an educator, I have found that *Sara Triumphant!* is an excellent text for teaching the events of the Holocaust by studying the individual experiences of a survivor. Sara's heart wrenching story is told with openness and honesty. It seamlessly blends historical facts with personal experience, thereby providing the reader with an account which is both accurate and moving. Students will connect with the humanity of this memoir. It is not only a documentation of the Holocaust; it is also a beautiful love story and a testament to the resilience of the human spirit.
— Professor Judith Vogel, The Richard Stockton College of NJ

A remarkable teenaged girl survives unimaginable horrors and emerges from the Holocaust to be swept up in a deeply moving love story— Sarah Paul is an inspiration for us all. A mesmerizing, unforgettable story!
— Bethanie Gorny, Ed.D., Author of *Fridays with Eva*,
past president of Jewish Family Services of Atlantic County, NJ,
and board member of the Stockton College of New Jersey Holocaust Resource Center.

Sara Triumphant!
Survivor of the Shoah

Ernest Paul
and Maryann McLoughlin

A Project of The Richard Stockton College of New Jersey
Sara & Sam Schoffer Holocaust Resource Center and
Graphics Production

COMTEQ PUBLISHING
MARGATE, NEW JERSEY

STOCKTON COLLEGE

THE RICHARD STOCKTON COLLEGE OF NEW JERSEY

**NEW JERSEY'S
GREEN COLLEGE®**

Stockton College is an AA/EO institution.

Published by:

ComteQ Publishing

A division of ComteQ Communications, LLC

101 N. Washington Ave. • Suite 2B

Margate, New Jersey 08402

609-487-9000 • Fax 609-487-9099

Email: publisher@comteqpublishing.com

Website: www.ComteQpublishing.com

ISBN 978-1-935232-09-4

Library of Congress Control Number: 2009933201

Book/Cover Design by Sarah Messina, Stockton Graphics Production

Endnotes and Discussion Questions by Maryann McLoughlin

Printed in the United States of America

10 9 8 7 6 5 4 3 2

This memoir is based on an April 5, 1996, interview in New York, filmed by the
Shoah Foundation, and on testimony from Sara Paul's husband,
Ernest Paul, also a Holocaust survivor.

Editor's Note

In some of the chapters that narrate the time after Ernest met Sara, there are two narratives of events—Sara's and Ernest's. Of course they are similar and may seem repetitious, but we felt it was important to include both. Each has some different details that we felt would be interesting to readers.

Maryann McLoughlin

June 2009

Dedication

To My Dear Family—
My Children:
My daughter, Dahlia;
my son Stewart and daughter-in-law, Nancy;
my son Gil and daughter-in-law, Dali

My Grandchildren:
Tara, Ilana, Ari, Eitan, Elite, and Daniel

Our Great Grandchildren:
Jake, Roman, Cole, Sean, Ryan Sara

In memory of my wife, Sara—
Your mother, your mom-mom, Savta Sara

I am dedicating this book to all of you—
I am grateful for your encouragement
in bringing this book to press
as a legacy and a true account.

Acknowledgements

I would like to thank my family for their love, support, and their encouragement to write Sara's memoir, especially Nancy and Stewart Paul for their help in coordinating the photographs and some of the letters and stories.

I appreciate all the help that was given to me by The Richard Stockton College of New Jersey. From the college's president, Dr. Herman Saatkamp, to the Dean of the College of General Studies, Dr. G. Jan Colijn, to the Director of the Holocaust Resource Center, Gail Rosenthal, all have been very supportive of projects for Holocaust survivors.

The publishing of this memoir was a team project: Leonard Pough of my company typed new chapters; Dr. Maryann McLoughlin, of Stockton's Holocaust Resource Center, transcribed Sara's Shoah Foundation oral history and edited the manuscript; Holocaust Resource Center interns, Kelsey Schneider and Stephanie Anderson, typed some of the additions such as the recipe section and the eulogies. Sarah Messina of Stockton's Graphics Production designed the cover and the book layout.

Thank you to everyone.

Ernest Paul April 2009

Note about Ernest Paul

Ernest Paul, Sara's husband, is also a Holocaust survivor. He is a survivor of Hungary where he was a member of the Hungarian resistance. In 2004, Mr. Paul was decorated by the Hungarian government for bravery and courage during the Holocaust.

Ernest is presently writing his memoir about the Hungarian underground and about his life after the Holocaust and his international business experiences. His memoir will be published in 2010.

Ernest Paul 2009
Photo by Margot Alten

Mother of My Heart: Dahlia's Preface

The greatest gift I ever received was my mother. As I reflect upon our relationship I believe she was my greatest inspiration and I hope I have made her proud by how I am living my life, by following her example. My mother exemplified the most wonderful qualities that anyone could possess. Her wisdom, compassion, and strength have guided me through the good times and bad. There was never an obstacle I encountered that was too large for mom to help me with.

If I was going through a tough time, mom would always get me through it with her advice, her support, or her great sense of humor. I miss all of our talks. I could talk to her about anything and I never felt judged. All I could feel was my mom's love.

I will always remember her kindness and loyalty to not only her family, but to her friends and often to strangers as well. Mom made an impression on everyone she touched, and they will never forget her generosity.

One of mom's greatest gifts to me was her courage and her will to live life to the fullest. As she battled her illness, I learned many great lessons. She woke up everyday with a positive attitude, and she taught me to always see the glass as half full.

Her determination to survive long enough to spend time with, and most importantly, to cook for, another generation, her great-grandchildren, truly was an inspiration.

I will miss all of our fun times together, whether it was our phone conversations (five times a day), shopping, working out, movies, lunches, and our times at the shore.

These times were always special to me. I'll never forget how dad would tease us about how we had to spend those times together to bond, and bond we did.

I was truly fortunate to have such an amazing mom; there will never be a better mom, grand mom, or great-grand mom than my mom, my role model.

I will miss her every day for the rest of my life.

Mom, as you always ended our conversations, this is from the "daughter of your heart."

ALL MY LOVE,
Dahlia May 2009

Nancy's Preface

I often thought of my mother-in-law's chosen hair color as an "I am Woman, Hear Me Roar" shade of red that revealed her inner strength and determination. It fairly shouted that she not only survived Hitler's war, but also was proud of her accomplishments in her beloved America. The red hair was her crown, given to herself, and worn with pride.

My mother-in-law was full of life; she enjoyed people and could be counted on to roll up her sleeves and join in any activity – whether play sword fighting with her grandsons, helping me address *Bar Mitzvah* invitations, or baking a cake for my neighbors. Hers was a resilient spirit; in spite of everything she had lived through during the *Shoah*, she embraced the world and was not a bitter person. In fact, she embodied love.

I marveled at my mother-in-law's ability to love after enduring the horrors of the war. She could have come out of the experience full of anger but she chose to embrace life with a generous spirit that was inspiring to all who knew her. She had a smile, a kind word, and the need to share her story with everyone she met. Her motto was, "Where there's life, there's hope," and she was proof of that.

Sara's need to tell her story helped to educate many about the horrors of war and the tragic price of intolerance and prejudice. It was as if the wounds inflicted during the Shoah continued to ooze, revealing themselves in the sad stories she continually told. Even happy occasions, such as a grandson's receiving special recognition for his award-winning writing, would remind her of all the talents and potential contributions destroyed before they had a chance to illuminate the world.

My mother and father-in-law, Sara and Ernest, came to America with their new little family in the late 1950s, just after I was born. One landsman would reach out a hand to help another come over until there were enough of them to call themselves "The New Americans." They were so proud to become American citizens.

The "New Americans" became family to each other, each one having lost so many loved ones during Hitler's war. The men worked very hard to provide for their growing families. Arriving without higher education or savings, they truly lived the American Dream and established themselves as successful businessmen and women through their sheer effort and drive.

The women were wonderful mothers who cherished not only their own children but also each other's children. They were advised by their children's teachers to speak only English at home and so they learned America's language along with their children. My mother-in-law worked alongside my father-in-law, volunteered at the children's schools and enthusiastically embraced all that America offered.

The "New Americans" celebrated everything together from birthday parties for the youngest children to college graduations and eventual weddings. In between the formal celebrations there were picnics and dances to raise money for different charities and over fifty summers together at the Jersey shore. There were card parties and bowling outings and many trips to take visiting friends to see the Liberty Bell and the Statue of Liberty. They loved showing off their America.

Then there was the food; mouth-watering dishes from Czechoslovakia, Hungary, Romania, and Israel showed up everywhere we gathered – including those car rides to show off America. Even Thanksgiving dinners featured humus, chicken soup with matzah balls and strudel for dessert. Everything was offered up in abundance. My mother-in-law said that feeding people was like therapy for her. She had two refrigerators stocked to bursting at all times – starvation's legacy. Everything was home-made and served with the utmost joy. My mother-in-law embraced Tupperware, making sure to send her special dishes to her married children's homes on a regular basis. Complete brunches and dinners would arrive at the Princeton Junction train station in a suitcase. *Rosh HaShanah* and Passover holiday feasts for the whole clan would require many duffle bags and a car service from Manhattan. Her Passover matzah cake was miraculous, ranking right up there with the manna from heaven and the parting of the Red Sea. There was always enough food to have leftovers for days, to fill our freezers, to share with our friends and neighbors. My mother-in-law loved nothing better than for us to gather under one roof to celebrate our traditions. Family was everything.

When my mother-in-law was liberated from Auschwitz, she was so sick and frail she was told that she would never be able to have children. Her three children were her miracles. Her six grandchildren were her hope for a brighter future without hatred, and she felt that her five great-grandchildren were her triumph over Hitler's effort to wipe out the Jewish people. She said that not until the great-grandchildren came did she finally find the smallest measure of peace, after a lifetime haunted by memories that disturbed her nights, even in golden America.

We spoke everyday about everything and nothing. We weren't beyond a little gossip now and again but we especially loved to talk about her "amazing" grandchildren and great-grandchildren, books, religion, philosophy, politics, nutrition, and fashion.

My mother-in-law dressed with a quiet elegance once she started to enjoy some financial success. She walked with her head held high, the epitome of dignity. I sometimes wondered if her great stylish flair didn't have more to do with remembering her nakedness in the concentration camps and wishing to cover the stain of Hitler's humiliation than with wanting to be a fashion maven.

Sara was much more to me than my mother-in-law. She was a loving mother, best friend, and teacher – she was truly a blessing in my life, inspiring me continually with her resilience and hopefulness. It was a privilege to have been able to call her "Ima." I loved her dearly and miss her more than words can say.

I never thought of my Ima as a Holocaust survivor. To me she was "Sara, Triumphant" – smart, savvy, sassy, and very strong.

Nancy Z. Paul

February 2009

Several ideas expressed in this preface have appeared in my article "At Passover, Remembering 'A New American,'" and are reprinted with permission from *The Princeton Packet*, April 18, 2008, 15A.

So you are
for me today, in the seagreen
sky, the greenery and
the leaf-rustling wind. I feel
you in every shadow, every movement,
and you put the world around me
like your arms. I feel the world
as your body, you look into my eyes
and call me with the whole world.

—Tadeusz Borowski, From "The Sun of Auschwitz"

Table of Contents

Part Two

Maps

Czechoslovakia, 1928: Sara lived in the Slovakia section.

images.google.com

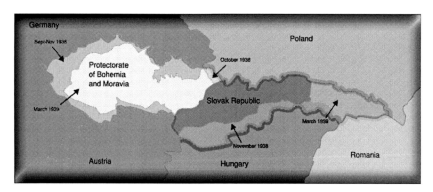

Partition of Czechoslovakia, 1938-1939, before WWII began.

images.google.com

Czechoslovakia—post WW II sfpa.sk/dokumenty/publikacie/22

Map of Concentration Camps: Concentration camps are marked with swastika; death camps are marked with a skeleton; and capital cities are marked with a star. Sara and her family were deported to Auschwitz-Birkenau Concentration Camp.
Sara was later sent to Stutthof. geocities.com.

Italy where Sara lived before immigrating to Israel.
images.google.com

Israel—modern map; Haifa where Sara and Ernest lived is circled.
itradio.org

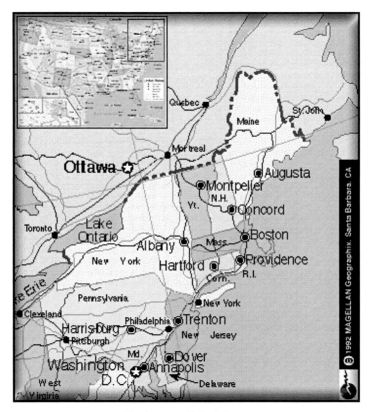

Northeastern United States
images.google.com

Part One

The chapters in Part One are based on
the Shoah Foundation interview
with Sara Paul in New York on April 5, 1996.

·· Chapter 1 ··

Two of The Lost

For fifty years I did not remember that I had two brothers. In 1994 I began, for the first time, to tell my story. I had a very difficult time talking about the Holocaust.

We began by recording my story on tape. As I talked and as time went on, two faces appeared—two little boys. These boys had on gray jackets with short pants and were wearing little hats. I thought perhaps they were cousins or next-door neighbors. Those little faces haunted me. One morning when I woke up two names popped up: Nahum and Velvel. I went to my husband, Ernest, and asked him if he had heard those names before. He said, "No." I asked him if I had ever said those names in my sleep. "No," again, was his answer. I asked my sons. Their response was the same as their father's—"No." No one had ever heard me name those names. My heart ached; I felt love for those boys.

I called my cousin, who had six siblings, and asked her, "Do you have brothers named Nahum and Velvel?" She said no. I then called my aunt and uncle living in Israel and asked them if they knew those two names. They said, "Sara, I think you had brothers by those names. But call your first cousin Chana in Israel. She lived close to you." We had gone to visit Chana and her family each summer.

So I called Chana. I asked her and she said, "Sara, you had brothers named Nahum and Velvel." In shock, I replied, "I didn't!" She repeated, "Yes, you did." Chana said, "I taught you and your brothers to ride your bikes."

I started to cry and ask, "Why did no one tell me that I had two brothers?" My cousin, asked, as if she were accusing me, "You don't remember your brothers?" I said, "No, and I don't know how they died." I was in terrible pain.

Chana told me to call Rifka, my friend from Krivé. She said, "Rifka was on the same cattle train as you and your two brothers." I called Rivka. She was happy to talk. She said, "Yes, you had two brothers. As we came down from the train they died a terrible death." I said, "Tell me. I have to know. For fifty years I didn't know that they existed. Tell me. My children don't know that I had brothers." Finally by my begging her, Rifka then told me of our arrival at the concentration camp:

Your older brother, Nahum, was very smart. He was especially good in math. He helped the other school kids solve their math problems. However, he was hard of hearing.

Your younger brother, Velvel, was only ten years old. All of us were in the cattle train. In fact, the whole cattle train was family. Your mother, grandpa, and great grandpa were with us.

When the train stopped, the doors opened. Outside were SS and black, ferocious-looking dogs. Your big brother was helping Velvel to get out. The SS began yelling, "Schnell! Schnell!" (Hurry! Hurry!) However, Nahum did not hear them; his back was to them as he assisted the little one. The SS stabbed him and stabbed him and when he fell they let the dogs on him. Velvel tried to help Nahum, but he also was stabbed and set on by the dogs. Then the SS pushed their bodies under the train, onto the tracks. You tried to help them but the SS pushed you away, hitting you on the head.

Only one of my uncles was left alive. He never asked me what happened to Nachem and Velvel. My uncle thought that I didn't want to talk about it. My uncle felt that because this was so painful to me, then why bring it up. I called everyone I knew—"Tell me about them." My family has been very supportive. They told me that they would tell my brothers' names to their children.

I never said a prayer for them. I never lit a candle. I cannot remember them. I have no memory of their living at home. I only have their names. My pain was for not remembering them—as if I had killed them myself.

I went to my spiritual advisor, Rabbi Shrem of Sutton Place Congregation in New York. He is a very wise man. He said that I had put them out of mind because of what I had seen in the concentration camp. I lost my past with them. I had two brothers but I can't find them. He said that perhaps I am very lucky that I don't remember how they were killed. I still feel guilt: How could I have left them go? So these are the two brothers that I had. This is my most recent pain—after over fifty years.

Nancy, my daughter-in-law, told me that she would join me in lighting a *yahrzeit* candle (commemoration) and saying *Kaddish* (prayer of remembrance). She told me that it was not too late to say *Kaddish*. Nancy comforted me, suggesting that I was only able to survive psychologically by believing that I was an only child. But I was so sad, shocked, and full of guilt that Nancy found a psychiatrist who specialized in Holocaust grief and trauma. He tried to console me by explaining that to protect myself my mind had repressed the memory of my brothers, allowing me to survive my harrowing experiences and all my losses. I met with him only once, but Nancy and I continued to light remembrance candles, which helped ease my pain.

Chapter 2

*Legacy of Ba'al Shem Tov**

Three hundred years ago in Krivé, a village in the land of Slovakia, people awoke early on spring mornings, as they had for hundreds of spring times past, to the scent of cherry blossoms and apple trees, walnut and chestnut trees flowering in gardens and along cobbled streets; children awoke from dreams of the forest where they would go to pluck big brown mushrooms, where blueberry, strawberry and raspberry bushes grew lush, and the forest stood only an hour's walk from the nearby Carpathian Mountains, wreathed in silent mists of dawn on the eastern border of Krivé. The Tisa River flowed through the valley in the center of town, reached on both sides by steps, crossed here and there by small wooden bridges.1 The muted song of rushing mountain water rose in the still morning air to Upschitzer Street, which lay parallel to the Tisa.

Of all the town's inhabitants none greeted each day more fully aware of the perfect natural beauty which was their home, nor lived with more gratitude for the harmony of life here than those who resided on Upschitzer Street.

* Some of the prose in chapters 2, 3, 6 comes from a version of Sara's story prepared by Frances in 1996. That version was never published.

In the year 1700, on the other side of the Carpathian Mountains, in Ukraine, was born Israel ben Eliezer, the Ba'al Shem Tov, Master of the Good Name, who is said, by the age of twelve, to have seen the hidden mysteries of the Torah, and who possessed the ability to incorporate this wisdom into his daily life in such a way as to inspire Jews to come and sit by him, observe his ways, and hush in reverent silence as he imparted wisdom. 2 It is said of the Ba'al Shem Tov that when he lifted his spoon for midday soup all those present observed in wonder, for he neither inclined toward the bowl nor spilled even a drop into his full beard of autumn gold. For sharing of wisdom and for habits of cleanliness and piety, the Ba'al Shem Tov might have earned sufficient merit for his years. But his name continues to be revered for his great accomplishment of bringing renewed energy and vitality to Judaism; he encouraged rejoicing, celebration of the Lord's Kingdom in heaven and on earth, and under his guidance Jews became newly awakened to the voice of God. For their absolute immersion in pietism these Jews came to be known as Hasidim.

The legacy of the Ba'al Shem Tov's inspired teaching passed on from his disciples to generations of descendants. His teachings traveled with them and as the decades passed Hasidic dynasties became established throughout all of Eastern Europe.

Hasidism spread even to Slovakia, which on October 28, 1918, joined with Bohemia, Moravia, Silesia and Sub Carpathian Ruthenia to establish the Czechoslovak Republic.

In the year 1930 there lived in Krivé seven-hundred Jewish families, three-hundred descended from Hasidic dynasties begun by the Ba'al Shem Tov. On Upschitzer Street, Bella Kafmanova, age twenty, a young woman of elegance, grace, and rare blond beauty, wife of Shlomo, brought a daughter into the world and named her Sara.

According to custom, Bella's father presented to the newborn baby a pair of little earrings, beautifully set rubies encircled by white diamonds, and next door in Grandmother Rivka's house, a crowd of relatives celebrated the occasion as the earrings were locked into the tiny lobes of Sara's ears. Eight grandparents and great-grandparents were in attendance from both sides of the family, as were the sisters of Bella and Shlomo, numerous aunts and uncles, and cousins of every age. Grandmother Rivka, wisps of russet hair escaping from under a headscarf tied in back, had been busy all week, roasting geese and chickens, and baking sponge cake and apple strudel in anticipation of this joyful day.

From the beginning of her life Sara was dearly loved. She'd been born into an exceedingly loving family and to a mother who'd longed for a daughter, for Rivka had often confided in Bella, "Bella, my precious daughter, I pray that God will bless you with a daughter, just as He blessed me with you."

Chapter 3

Childhood

My hometown was Uličské Krivé, in Czechoslovakia (present day, Ukraine), where I was born on June 1, 1929. My father, whose name was Shlomo, was born in Vilvis on April 18, 1899. My mother, Bella (Beyla) was born on August 15, 1901. In Europe at that time the couple did not go to city hall to have wedding papers. All they needed was a rabbi and a *Chuppah*, and they were married.[3]

My father worked with diamonds and precious stones. He had learned his profession in Belgium where he was taught how to cut and polish diamonds.[4] He knew how to solve problems such as split stones; he was considered a master diamond cutter. He often traveled to Budapest, Hungary, and to other big cities such as Vienna in Austria. He went by carriage and horses to the station and then caught the train. Even with father traveling, mother was never alone, but was supported by family.

I had a wonderful childhood, surrounded by love from my parents and my grandparents on both sides—from 200 family members, including the second and third generations. In Eastern Europe in those days families were very close and helped each other. If someone had a problem, there was a gathering to decide how to help him or her.

I remember we had a record player; they called them gramophones then.[5] We had four records. We used to play the music, opening wide the windows and doors so our neighbors could hear. In our town everybody was friendly to the neighbors. I felt the constant love.

I remember laughter, lots of laughter. I remember the smells of the *Shabbos* meals. My family was religious; therefore, we had prayers every Friday night. Friday night was very beautiful with the prayers and the family getting together. My uncles and aunts lived four streets away. There were lots of places to go. I had a secure feeling: so many people loved me. I remember picnics. I would pick mushrooms, strawberries, and raspberries. The cousins would go in groups with little buckets. Mine would fill up quickly.

I remember the excitement on holidays. Everyone came home. Everybody was given little presents. Two times a year we received new clothes, in the spring and in the summer. For Passover (*Pesach*) I remember patent leather shoes that I loved and a new dress.[6]

In the town were three synagogues, three churches, and two schools. There were huge chestnut trees along the streets with flower gardens in the front of the houses and vegetable gardens in the back. To the east, mountains were above us.

My grandparents and great-grandparents always made me toys and clothes. I remember my great-grandfather made a sled by hand. While I watched him work, he polished the runners with candle wax and soap, explaining patiently that this was how to insure a smooth ride down the mountain, always maintaining clean and polished runners. I had my own skis, which I used to polish. Another great-grandfather, Shaynya's husband, made my dollhouses. I remember the dollhouse he made for me and the hours he sat by the fire on winter nights carving miniature beds and tables and chairs. The great-grandmothers fashioned dolls for me, using rags, old stockings and socks, painting on the mouths, and sewing on buttons for eyes.

My grandmother, Rivka, sewed my dresses. She possessed an uncommon talent for dressmaking. Although many women in Krivé would have liked Rivka to sew for them, she fashioned dresses exclusively for her granddaughters, often working with velvet, her favorite fabric, and trimming the dresses with her own hand crocheted collars, adding here and there a needle point flower. Except for the buttons and ruffles and bows that Rivka occasionally felt inspired to add, I loved the dresses my grandmother sewed for me.

If I wanted to "fix" a dress by removing a ruffle or something else, Bella would never permit it: "Your grandmother went to the trouble of buying such beautiful material and then she sat for hours to make you a dress. This you want to change? No, Sara. Your grandmother made it and it's beautiful, and you should love it because you're lucky to have such a grandmother."

One great-grandmother, Shaynya, had a tradition. All her great-grandchildren would sit down around her. Her pockets were always filled with dates, figs, and imported walnuts. Then she read to us from a book. She told us all those stories about Esther and Ruth. She made them very interesting. After this we had tea and latkes. Then our parents came to join us for tea.

Adjacent to my school lived my Aunt Sara, who had two grown children. She owned a small dairy factory where she made cottage cheese and sour cream. During morning recess, Aunt Sara brought me fresh bread and sweet, fresh butter and sometimes grapes from her garden. We would sit close together on an old tree stump and eat and talk. "Eat, Sarale, eat," Aunt Sara would beg. "What am I going to do with you? You eat like a little bird." Often I shared bread and butter with my friend, Anna.

That was a warm and loving kind of life.

I remember hopscotch. In my mind's eye, I see the other girls in their starched little dresses, jumping rope and playing with me. A quite beautiful life—people cared for each other very much.

We had many non-Jewish neighbors—they had lived generations with us in the same city. We didn't consider them as another religion or race. They had different holidays. We had Passover; they had Easter. They had Christmas; we, Hanukkah.[7] We went to school together. We played together and lived together very nicely. My grandmother said that people have to live together because they are involved with each other like an orchestra. The orchestra needs the piano, the drums, the violin, etc. Imagine if we took away the piano. How would the orchestra sound? She said, "We need every one."

Unhappily, in the churches, from the time they were little, non-Jews had been taught that the Jews had killed their Christ—Jesus. What did we have to do with that? Nonetheless, we lived in peace with them. They went to church. We went to synagogue. There was never any incident. I have no recollection of any conflicts. We were orthodox; however, some were more religious than others.[8] When I went to visit the Meshulam, my cousin, an Orthodox rabbi, I could not have short sleeves or short socks. I had to cover my knees and wear long socks.

Our town had Hasidic Jews.[9] They had many students that went to *yeshiva*,[10] a school that teaches *Torah*, *Mishnah*, and *Talmud*.[11] These boys didn't have a place to live. Therefore, every night they ate in someone's house. Four days a week we fed the students, the poor, or the mentally ill. There were no institutions for the mentally ill. We adopted two and fed them: Hanter and Sander. They told people they met to go to Beyla's house—my mother's. They told them how good she was to them. When they came, she would seat them in the pantry. A maid saw that they were clean; then she dressed them and fed them soup.

We put aside Friday night, *Shabbat* evening, for travelers. There were seven or eight in our immediate family. This number would always double on Sabbath. People were brought home and we fed them.

There was one sorrow in my life. My father, Shlomo, died when I was two years old. I heard the story from my mother many times:

> Shlomo's ability as a cutter of large diamonds was sought after by diamond merchants in Berlin, Vienna, Budapest, wherever a special diamond required the skill of a master. One morning, while occupied with a brilliant blue-white diamond, a splinter pierced the second finger of Shlomo's right hand. A surgeon removed the splinter but microscopic particles of poison already swam in his bloodstream.

Shlomo's death felt to my mother like an earthquake; she felt her world had flattened.

No longer did the zest for life sparkle in in my mother's eyes nor lighten her step as she went about her daily routine. When she heard the sound of laughter she wondered, "How can they laugh? How can there be happiness anywhere with Shlomo gone?" To her the sound of laughter felt like a blow to her body or a slap across her face. Even the beauty of sunsets or flowering vines, which distinguished the Jewish houses, felt to my mother like an affront.

When I was older, my mother often described to me the many lovable, clever and unique aspects of Shlomo's personality, his dark hair styled short and modern, his tall slim frame and striking features. "Like a Greek sculpture," Mother said. Hungry for every word about my father, I begged for even more description, "Compare him to someone I know." mother would answer, "There is no one to compare. Your father was the handsomest man in the whole wide world."

"What about Yossi Mayer, my uncle?" I prodded. "Oh, yes. Yossi Mayer is a handsome man, but your father was so much more in every way, and so highly educated in *Torah*." Then mother would describe even the soft voice of her beloved husband.

Because of my mother's descriptions, I felt as if I knew my father even better than I knew my mother. The father I lost lived on in my imagination as a vibrant man who glowed with life, while my mother remained a sad and graceful beauty.

However, my childhood was not just stories and playing, I went to school five days a week. It had been established that we didn't have to go to school on Saturday and Sunday.

I went to public school. We said one prayer in the morning. I did not have to say this prater, however. I only had to bow my head and I could say any prayer that I wanted to say. In the morning, when we walked in, we said good morning to the teacher and sat down with bent heads and prayed. I accepted this as a part of my day.

I had an uncle, Uncle Chanoch, a Hebrew teacher. He taught *cheder*.[12] My uncle took three of his nieces and gave us private lessons. We learned to read and write in Hebrew. This was unusual; girls weren't generally taught Hebrew. But I was lucky. He did this for the rest of the girls too. Everyone I knew, including my mother, could read and write *Loshan Kodesh*, which is similar to Hebrew, but is the holy language of the bible.

I was encouraged and proud of myself when I came to the Passover *Seder*, the feast commemorating the exodus of the Jews from Egypt, celebrated on the first night of Passover. I did understand. I knew why we had matzah and that we had been enslaved in Egypt.[13]

For the Passover gathering we opened up three rooms. There were no long tables, but we made legs and covered them with boards covered with linen sheets. My great-grandfather, Chainach, put on his *kittel* (his white linen robe), and presided over *Seders*.[14] Majestic, he reclined on a high bench cushioned with colorful pillows.

Nowadays there are not many who attend our Passover. Not even twenty-four. It is different. Things have changed. Yet I look around and see my children. To see those faces makes me happy. I feel also the presence of the others. I guess this is the reason I survived—to remember those faces and those happier times.

Chapter 4

Peace Disrupted

In our town there were four or five radios. We had one. However, the first time we heard about Hitler and the trouble Jews were having, it was hearsay. We heard they were beating Jews here and there. Actually we were used to hearing about antisemitism. We lived close to Russia and Poland. We had heard about the Cossacks and the pogroms.[15] In times past, reports had reached Upschitzer Street of pogroms in Russia where Cossacks on horseback, with the ferocity of beasts, had thundered into peaceful *shtetls* murdering Jews, wrecking and torching Jewish homes, raping and slashing Jewish daughters. The Cossacks would tie Jews to their horses and ride around the *shtetls* dragging Jews behind them. The Jews of Krivé were accustomed to worrying, but they said, "Such things could never happen here."

The Kiev pogroms of 1919 by the Cossacks proved the first of up to 2,000 pogroms that took place in the Ukraine alone. The pogroms were marked by utmost cruelty and face-to-face brutality. Thousands of women were raped. Hundreds of *shtetlach* were pillaged, and Jewish neighborhoods were left in ruins. According to some estimates, overall, in the pogroms of 1918-1921, half a million Jews were left homeless. (en.wikipedia.org)

On November 10, 1938 we heard news from Germany of *Kristallnacht* (The November Pogrom) in Germany and Austria.[16] This news shattered the peace on Upschitzer Street. The previous evening Hitler's henchmen had stormed the streets of German and Austrian cities and villages. We heard that many Jewish men were beaten and killed, thousands were imprisoned, and synagogues were burned and destroyed. We heard also about the Brown Shirts and their violent behavior.[17] Jewish-owned property was ransacked and walls were marred with frightening ugliness: black swastikas, SS death-heads, *Juden Raus* (Jews Out).

Compelled by the news of *Kristallnacht*, and with deliberate urgency, my mother began to instruct me in the disciplined ways of housecleaning. She even constructed a small stool which enabled me to wash dishes at the kitchen sink. Mother did not usually speak in Yiddish; however, on that day, the day after the November Pogrom, when the family gathered next door at Grandmother Rivka's, she did. "I'm teaching you to be able to survive, *mein kind* (my child)." My mother's words seared into my memory. "My child, you must remember, whatever I have taught you till now you'll be able to use to survive."

Nervous and frightened, the adults gathered around the scrubbed oak kitchen table. I observed the constant motion of hands clasping and unclasping. Furrows and creases in their faces caught my attention. "How do we know they won't come here?"
"Here? Czechoslovakia? Never!"

Anxious glances were exchanged. The conflict between faith in the democratic government of their country and terror about destruction to which they saw themselves vulnerable weighted the atmosphere in Rivka's kitchen. The terrifying menace of Nazis looming over Krivé and searching every house for Jews—with boots! Rifles! Clubs! Never! Rivka's kitchen grew silent.

Great-grandmother Shaynya, as on every Sabbath, gathered the children who joined her on the brocade horsehair sofa. "Oh, look!" Shaynya exclaimed, determined not to deprive her twelve great-grandchildren of the game she played with them. "My pockets are so full! Would you look and see what's there?" Her pockets, as always, were stuffed with goodies, delicacies like dates, figs and walnuts. Laughing, the children crowded around Shaynya, reaching for her bulging pockets.

The sofa had been placed in this parlor when Shaynya's mother had been a bride, and the younger children sprawled cozily on the fine Persian carpet, which had belonged to Shaynya's grandmother. The family was accustomed to living among the fine, though worn, furnishings acquired by previous generations and handed down or bequeathed to newly married daughters and granddaughters. My great-grandmother opened the *siddur* (prayerbook) and prepared to translate from the Hebrew text as she read aloud. First, as she was accustomed to doing, her eyes lingered a moment on each child as in loving tones she reminded them of their roots, of how the cemetery held the remains of their ancestors going back six generations, of how many generations were descended from Rabbi Ba'al Shem Tov. The children felt loved and secure, surrounded by their family and their history. After prayers she read a Bible story, engaging our attention with her animated voice and her talent for dramatic gestures.

Gentile families also counted their generations in Czechoslovakia, and friendships among Jewish and non-Jewish families were common. Each year Christians invited to their homes for Christmas Eve three generations of Jewish friends. Czechoslovakia had elected to the presidency Eduard Benes, a Christian who as an orphaned child had been lovingly raised by a Jewish family.[18] To the Jews this appeared to be a clear affirmation of Czechoslovakia's democratic principles.

In March of 1939 peace was disrupted when Germany invaded Czechoslovakia;[19] President Benes fled to London where he set up a government-in-exile, and immediately, Hitler established a puppet government headed by Father Josef Tiso.[20] The Treaty of Protection was signed which made Slovakia, in effect, a satellite of Germany, and a reign of terror was unleashed against the Jewish community.[21] Mobs of previously law-abiding citizens wrecked and burned synagogues. Jewish cemeteries were desecrated. Jewish businesses were boycotted. Jews were dismissed from employment, rounded up in cafes and on public avenues, and deported to labor camps established in collaboration with the Slovak leadership.

Then war was declared on September 1, 1939.[22] The adults sat around the table and they were scared. This was the first fear that I had felt.

> Before World War II, 135,000 Jews lived in Slovakia; 5,000 of whom immigrated before the war. Under the protection of Nazi Germany, Slovakia proclaimed its independence in March 1939. The country came under the control of an extremely religious and right-wing party, the Hlinka (Slovak) Peoples' party, under the leadership of Father Jozef Tiso, a Catholic priest. After its establishment, the Slovakian government approached the "Jewish Question" as one of their first public issues.

> The first anti-Jewish law was passed in Slovakia on April 18, 1939. A few days later, on April 24, Jews were excluded from all government positions and service. On September 19, 1939, all Jews were expelled from the military. Many more discrimination laws followed, including children being ousted from school and Jews being excluded from public recreational facilities. By

1940, more than 6,000 Jews emigrated both legally and illegally. The Slovakian government passed a law that permitted it to take over control of all major Jewish businesses. These laws were supported by the majority of Slovakians.

In a 1940 meeting between German and Slovakian officials, Germany dictated new changes within the Slovakian government to make the country more dependent. During this period, Jews lost many more privileges, including the right to a car or gun. In August 1940 another decree was issued that required every Jew to register with the government and state their financial status.

On September 9, 1941, Jews were met with a proclamation of 270 articles, which included the wearing of a Yellow Star of David and forced labor. Soon after, Hungary and the Slovakian government began deporting the Jews to concentration camps, specifically Auschwitz. (jewishvirtuallibrary.org)

The Nazis created a government in Czechoslovakia and had their own people doing the dirty work. Then there were roundups. The local people helped. They knew who was a Jew and who did what. When those who for years had been nice to us turned against us and helped the Germans, we were shocked and hurt.

During this time, part of our family was sent to the Ukraine. They passed a law that if family members did not have papers—were not born in Czechoslovakia—they would be deported. The Germans and Hungarians came in and deported families that had no papers. It happened overnight, like a blitz. The families were sent to Kamenetz-Podolski. "One of the first and largest Holocaust mass-murder[s] occurred on August 27-28, 1941 near the city of Kamenetz-Podolski.

In those two days, 23,600 Jews were killed. This massacre was the first mass action in the 'final Solution' of the Nazis" (en.wikipedia.org).[23]

My cousin Sara Rasmovich's brother and sister were killed over in the Ukraine. Her parents took money and jewelry and bribed peasants to bring the rest of the family back under hay in their wagons. They crossed the border back into Czechoslovakia into another town.

In February of 1942 the Germans arrived in Krivé and they delivered to City Hall their official request for lists naming the Jews of Krivé. And the administrators complied with astonishing accuracy.

Gradually our rights were taken away. We found out that Jewish children were not allowed to go to school. We were not allowed to travel. We had to wear the yellow star with the word *Juda* written on it. We heard that other communities were being sent to ghettos.

How did we feed the family? Ours was a large family so some had farms and vineyards. We always had enough food.

However, by 1942 and 1943 there was already the Holocaust but without the crematoria—that came later for us.

By 1942, nearly three-fourths of the Slovakian Jewry had been murdered in Auschwitz. (jewishvirtuallibrary.org)

Chapter 5

Betrayal

In March 1943, a few weeks after their arrival in Krivé, Nazi troops advanced on Upschitzer Street, and the song of the Tisa River vanished in echoes of German boots marching to round up the Jews. I wore several sweaters under my coat and and wrapped myself in scarves knitted by aunts and grandmothers. My mother too was dressed warmly. With trembling hands, my mother fastened her camel-hair coat trimmed with fur. She wore a warm, Russian-style fur hat, and carried a fur muff. Boots of dark brown felt covered her legs. Tall, slim and blond, my mother was a strikingly beautiful woman. I was twelve years old then, walking beside my mother, holding hands, a dozen steps behind the Nazi escort, walking toward the train station.

Inside my coat pocket my fingers closed around the familiar crystal rock of salt, my treasure, a memento from a second grade class trip to the salt mines outside Krivé. With my classmates and teacher I had descended the carved salt steps to a cavern of salt deep beneath the earth's surface. The grownups predicted that one day the whole town, including its airport where three airplanes landed daily, would, because of the extensive mining, collapse into the earth. I saw that workers had carved into the crystal walls a sculpture of Jesus on the cross in detailed artistry. Pure and white, the cavern sparkled everywhere, and the cathedral-like ceiling caused my classmates and me to imagine we had arrived in Paradise. A whole city was built within this huge mountain of salt and at least a hundred men labored there. While we watched, the laborers carried chunks of salt packed in burlap bags up toward the surface, and my teacher explained that the mine was government-owned and that salt was an excellent product for exporting. That day each schoolchild was given a small bit of salt to take home and ever since I had saved mine, a precious piece of crystal, a tiny chunk of paradise, and this crystal I carried in my pocket, a memento of my beautiful childhood.

Gathered together were Aunt Sara, my mother's older sister; her husband, Uncle Chanoch who had taught me Hebrew; and their daughter and son, Meshulam, an Orthodox rabbi; Meshulam's wife with their four sons and three daughters; and another married son, Moishi, and his wife with their four sons and one daughter. Great-grandparents Chaindel and Kuppel, my mother's grandparents, and great-grandparents, Shaynya and Chanoch, my mother's other grandparents were with us. Great-grandfather Chainach was admired for his curly blond hair, smooth, fair skin, and blue eyes. Indelible in my mind was an image of my great-grandfather presiding over *Seders*.

I caught a glimpse of little Esther, my cousin, walking. All the cousins: Sosi, David, Salas, Rosci, Bisczi, Toby Hanah, Shlomo, Avraham, beautiful Hanya, were walking together. "Faster! Hurry!" The Nazi guards shouted, raising their truncheons. With exceeding thoroughness, they had rounded up every Jewish family in Krivé.

All around me I heard soft, muffled sobbing. I too was crying. I glanced at Grandma Rivka and saw that her eyes were filled with fear and anguish. She was weeping, straining to keep up with the swift pace. In the morning light Grandma Rivka's complexion, clear and unlined, was drained of all color. Grandma Rivka had never once scolded me, not even when I had taken her lovely embroidered silk bed jacket and had cut it apart to fashion for myself a little dress. The cousins had warned, "Grandmother will be angry! You will be punished." But Grandma Rivka, instead of scolding, had declared, "Oh! Look how talented you are! Sewing a beautiful dress!"

Aunt Sara was staring straight ahead as she maintained the pace alongside Grandma Rivka.

My maternal grandfather strode with long legs in leather boots, his yarmulke unseen under his Russian fur hat. Everything about him was dark, including his olive complexion, except for eyes of startlingly clear blue and his clean white shirt. I was close enough, however, to see tears on my grandfather's face, running silently into his beard.

Several paces back and to the right I saw my great-grandfather, Rivka's father, walking with his usual dignified carriage, his blue eyes watering. I glimpsed another great-grandfather, Shaynya's husband, Chanoch, who strode with a strong, military posture, his gaze fixed and steady.

As we marched down the middle of the street, everyone was weeping, holding children's hands, clutching babies close, carrying bundles, carrying a minimum of possessions—some grain, oil, cooking pot, and a change of clothing. Only twenty-five kilos was permitted, so we carried mostly food, hurrying to keep the brisk pace the soldiers set.

Neighbors and friends emerged from doorways, lined the streets, watching as the Jews were taken from Krivé. What thoughts entered their minds at this scene? Neighbors had referred admiringly to Shaynya as "the Major," because of her perfect posture. But not now. At least not aloud. Perhaps the neighbors' vision was not focused on compassion for this terrible ordeal the Jews were facing. They may have instead been thinking of digging up buried Jewish belongings. Whispered rumors, brought to synagogue by a Jew who escaped deportation had prompted many Jews, my mother among them, to gather their brass and silver possessions and their jewelry, and, with the help of trusted neighbors, to bury their valuables for safekeeping.

Their greed was stronger than their friendship!

Years later, after the war was over, survivors returning to reclaim possessions learned that even before the train carrying the Jews away had rounded the curve of the railroad tracks, these neighbors had rushed to unearth the hidden valuables. Even before the cold March sun had given way to a wicked night, there had been such a frenzy of looting and arguing and tearing from each other's hands as to mark the day well in the collective memory of Krivé. Jewish goose feather pillows, Jewish coats, dresses, suits, and scarves, Jewish armoires and carpets were spirited away to their neighbors' houses. By sunrise of the next day families awoke in Jewish beds and breakfasted at Jewish tables. Jewish homes had already been claimed by Christian families. Survivors were told that some people became so embittered by their swifter neighbors' usurping coveted property that rifts continued for decades.

On the corner, by the bakery, stood a group of my classmates. I saw Anna, my best friend, with whom I had often shared a warm slice of bread spread with sweet butter; she stuck out her tongue at me. Another friend, Geiza, gathered there, too. They waved, smiled and clapped their hands, as they called out, "Goodbye, Jews!" The women, who had envied my mother's beauty as well as her fur-trimmed camel hair coat, smirked, smiled mean smiles, and turned their backs as she passed.

A burning pain of betrayal shot through my heart. I felt as if I was falling helplessly into an abyss. No more home. No school. No friends.

No one cared what happened to me even though yesterday my friends were in our kitchen eating strudel at our table.

I hurried. "Faster! Faster!" The soldiers kept shouting. The pain of betrayal burned in my heart, and my face, like the faces of my loved ones, was streaked with hot tears.

When they took us out of our homes, we lost not only our homes and material things but also our best fiends, those we thought were our best friends. Our security! We didn't know what was awaiting us. We thought we were going to slave labor. We didn't know about the concentration camps. The soldiers yelled, "Schnell! Schnell! (Quickly! Quickly!) We were surrounded by the soldiers and dogs.

As we came to the end of our city, we saw cattle trains waiting for us. The soldiers pushed in as many as they could, like sardines. Older people, new mothers with babies, the sick—they pushed us all in. Inside the cattle car were two tiny windows, very high up, one at one end and one at the other. This was the only air we had until they stopped and opened the door. We were locked in the darkness. They gave us two buckets and told us to use these if we needed to. In the middle of the night when we had to go, we had to push our way through to the bucket. When we stopped, they emptied the buckets. We could sit down. Small children sat on grandfathers' laps. We had our supplies, but we couldn't eat raw beans. We shared our food—our cakes and bread. There were only two buckets of water; we all had to share these. We had fresh water but not enough. We were not told where we were going. We had no idea where we were headed. We were about two days on the train. We arrived at Mátészalka, Hungary, which is about two hours away from Krivé.[24]

When they opened the train door, we were immediately surrounded by Hungarian and German soldiers. It was chaos. Pushing. Shoving. Many people with beards were pulled down and kicked. On our train were a dentist and doctor, friends; they had taken pills to commit suicide. They were lying in the car dead. They had planned this death.

ᚖ·· Chapter 6 ··ᚖ

Mátészalka Ghetto

After our arrival in Mátészalka, we were directed to a big tent that was the camp kitchen. We had to use our own food; the SS gave us nothing so we put our food together. In the camp kitchen, a tent, were four cooks and helpers who cooked with what they had—the many foodstuffs that everybody had brought. After it was cooked, the food was rationed out. We stood in line to receive our ration. After several weeks, they gave us post cards that they said they would mail for us. My cousin Zipporah had married three months earlier, but the couple had been separated. Her husband and her husband's oldest brother had been sent out as slave laborers for the military. So she wrote to her husband. She wrote how terrible her situation was and that she didn't know where she was going after the ghetto. She wrote also that she was living in a tent. Four other women wrote things like that. The Nazis read those post cards; then they built a platform and hanged these women by the arms and legs. Zipporah had to pour water on their faces so they would come to—to suffer more. Three survived this brutality, but they were never the same. We had to watch, a terrible thing. The Hungarians and the SS made sure that we looked. We were not allowed to bow our heads.

We were there for six weeks. As time passed there was less and less food. By now the ghetto held over two thousand people. Committees organized the food. We received less food—only once a day. Many died in the Mátészalka Ghetto. A mother was nursing her baby and there was nothing in her breast to nourish her baby. The oldest wanted to give their food to the youngest. The young ones felt guilty. In their weakened condition, many also died of fever. The Hungarians soldiers started a rumor that we would be sent to another place where they would kill us. We didn't believe them.

During this time they began transporting people. Slowly, slowly they were taking the people out of the ghetto. They selected people and took them to the station to the cattle trains. Hundreds and hundreds at a time were deported from the ghetto. These were the same trains that were transporting the military to the Eastern front.

My mother and I were on the last transport. There were beatings and again chaos! People started to believe that there was no way out— no escape. People were numb. They felt no hope; they were in despair. The train came—a long, long train with people from other ghettos. The Hungarian soldiers told us, "From where you are going you will not return. If you have valuables, give them to us. Leave them in your own country; don't take them to the Germans." We went into the cattle cars again. Only this time it was worse going into the cars because we knew what they were like—atrocious! The SS and Hungarian soldiers were in regular cars. We only saw them when we stopped. We needed them because they gave us bread and soup in buckets. We had those other buckets again, too—odorous. People were dying. Babies were crying. If a baby died, we heard the painful cry of the mother. We were filthy. We smelled. The buckets overflowed. They smelled. The stench!

My mother was a beautiful, elegant woman—blonde hair, black eyes, and a terrific figure. She was in one corner. I was with her and my grandparents. Mother developed a tooth infection. She was in agony but tried to hide the pain. I was scared. My great-grandfather had been separated from us. The cattle wagons were horrific: seeing people die, the dirt, the smell, the dead bodies!

After another two days, we arrived at our destination.

Chapter 7

Auschwitz-Birkenau

When the train stopped, they opened the doors. We had been in the dark for a long time. We were blinking because of the daylight. When we could see, we looked out and saw high electrical wires and military barracks. There were different Lagers—A, B, C. We saw people there with no hair. We saw women with ill-fitting dresses. People were milling around. My mother said to me, "This must be a military institution, and they must have brought us here to take care of these people.[25]

A number of Polish men and women had come to clean the trains and they whispered to us, "Say you are sixteen. Give the babies to your mothers and grandparents. Say you are seventeen or eighteen."

The SS said, *"Los! Los!"* (Let's go! Let's go!) My family clambered out of the train. Many others were lying inside, not getting up. They were my neighbors and friends. The pain was so strong that I was numb. As I climbed down from the train, they told me where to go. There was a narrow walkway. At the table were three Germans, Mengele and two others, with whom we came face to face. They said, *"Recht. Links. Recht. Links."* (Right. Left). Small children and grandparents went another way. I didn't look like a child; I had long hair and was already developed, so I was sent another way. My mother was at a distance in another line; beautiful women, gorgeous women, were there. To three sets of twins, six little girls, Mengele said, "Over there." To others he said, "You dirty, filthy Jews stay here." Cousins, neighbors, girlfriends were directed to the left. They were marched away.

Mothers didn't want to give up nursing babies, so the SS wrested the babies from their arms, putting them in the same trucks that had the suitcases. I saw the SS hit a three or four month old little baby against a telephone pole; brain matter came out of his little head. The mother was tearing her hair and trying to bite the SS. The SS took their babies no matter how much the mothers cried. They threw them like potatoes into trucks. Beautiful babies! And their mothers had to watch all of this. Such heartrending cries! I was only thirteen. How could anyone do this? They had no feeling. On their faces were sadistic smiles. They didn't even use bullets. Bullets were too precious; they were needed for the war. They stabbed and bayoneted. The trucks came. The babies went. The mothers were taken away.

I didn't see my mother anymore. My cousins were to one side. "Don't tell them we are related; they will divide us up." The young people were taken to Lager C. I was standing by myself, not knowing what was going on. Then I was put in a group.

This group was sent to a place where old men with beards were waiting for us. They told us to take our clothes off. We stood there naked. People searched us inside and outside, looking for diamonds. If they found anything, they ripped it out. They ripped out the ruby and diamond earrings that my father had given me when I was two years old. They were all that I had left of my father!

Then they cut everybody's hair. We didn't know who was who. They put me with the twins. They told me that I was going to be a messenger. They gave us dresses—short dresses on tall; long dresses on short. Our shoes didn't fit.

I was sent to Lager C, 32 Block. Wooden boards had been shoved into this block, but there was no place to lie down. They had no time to build the bunks. The floor was muddy; nonetheless, people were lying on the ground. Our *Stubenälteste* (barrack leader) Magda, a Slovaki Jew, had been there many years. She was wearing wooden clogs, and to punish us, she would hit us on the head with a clog. A mother with two daughters was spitting up blood. Magda hit her so many times that she fell and died. She said, "I am here three years already. See what they have done to me! I have pieces of flesh missing because I tried to run away and they set the dogs on me. Luckily a Polish doctor helped to heal my wounds. You think you have it bad? There are no dogs on you." On the third day, I realized that the chimneys were smoking all the time. I smelled a barbeque smell. None of us knew.

I was lying there but at 3:00 AM, I was woken for *Appell* (Roll call).[26] The SS wanted to count us. We had to stand five in a row. If people were missing, I, as messenger, had to go to another block and ask for "pieces—sticks." We had to stand there until the SS were ready. After they had breakfast; they looked us over to select for the gas chambers. I would pinch and pinch my cheeks to make them red, and I would stand straighter. The people who were not looking healthy were taken aside and away with the SS yelling, "Raus! Raus!" If a mother had two daughters, one was taken away. There were always many, many people pulled out. We couldn't do anything. We couldn't understand not just what they did but why they did it.

One morning, after *Appell*, we were with the people cleaning the trains. I asked one *Stubendienst* (barrack supervisor), who watched us, beat us, and stole from us, "I want to find out where my mother, cousins, and aunts are." She replied, "Come. I'll show you." Five crematoria were blazing. From out of the chimneys came a rainbow. I couldn't stand the barbeque smell. She asked, "When did you arrive?"

I said, "A week ago."

She said, "They have long, long, been ashes."

I asked, "What do you mean?"

She said, "The gas. The ovens. When dead, they pick out the golden teeth."

I asked, "And the rainbow?"

She answered, "From the fat."

I continued asking, "Where is my family?"

She said, "Don't ask me any more questions."

Then she slapped me. People like her got better treatment from the SS if they were cruel to their charges. *Later in the sanatorium, I met Sandek, a Sonderkommando, who told me that he had put his own mother into the ovens.* [27] *He was in the sanatorium because his lungs were so bad from the gases he had inhaled.*

Chapter 8

Appell at Auschwitz

Every morning, at *Appell*, we would spend four or five hours standing and waiting—five to a row. There were 32, 000 in my camp alone. Every fifth person got a small loaf of bread that she would divide among the people in her row. Sometimes a person would get a bigger piece and then a fight would break out. We were given soup once a day. The kitchen workers put in rotten turnips or potatoes. They cooked dead horsemeat and rotten vegetables. They threw sand in so the soup was gritty. Each of us had a little tin dish. We couldn't lose this dish because if we lost it or someone stole it, we couldn't eat, not even this foul soup!

On the day we thought was *Yom Kippur* (Day of Atonement), although we weren't exactly sure of the day or time, we decided we were going to fast—whoever wanted to.[28] So the SS spilled the rest of the soup out on the ground. We fasted. The next evening the soup was spilled out again. They said, "If you are stupid enough to fast, then you'll get nothing until the next afternoon." At this time a new transport came in—Hungarians. One woman told us, "Yom Kippur is next week." We replied, "We fasted already."

We continued standing for *Appell* for four or five hours. We waited as they weeded out people. I had no hope. I was holding on as long as I could.

The camp was surrounded by electric wires. A mother lost a daughter; a daughter, her mother. I saw people sitting dead by the wires—suicides. Many, many people did this.[29]

In the camp was a Prima Donna from *The Teatro alla Scala*, or La Scala in Milano, Italia.[30] She was the only one who had her hair. We were surrounded by the SS. Around us were huge piles of stone. As we were breaking stones into small pieces for roads, she sang, her face dirty, streaked by tears tracing grooves in the dirt. The Prima Donna, with dirty hair and face, was sitting on a pile of stones, singing arias from *La Traviata* and *Aida*. We heard her song. The SS threw bread to her.

..🜂.. Chapter 9 ..🜂..

Mother

When I wasn't carrying messages, I was assigned to various *Kommandos* (work groups). Once I was assigned to a *Kommando* to clean out the trains after they had disgorged their passengers. This was a good assignment, one I was on for three months. When we went out of the gates, soldiers and dogs surrounded us. However, as we walked I could see the nearby trees. I loved to look at trees. They were so alive that they made me feel alive. As we walked, sometimes we were hit with a rifle or kicked with a boot. I tried to walk in the middle.

One day as we walked, I noticed a lot of dogs, and I saw naked bodies digging a huge pit. Among these, I saw my mother—but her eyes were dead. Despite this, somehow she winked at me so I would know her. It was terrible to see her naked in front of all the soldiers and other people. I wanted to give her my dress. I started toward her; however, my friend pulled me away. I heard shots. I must have blacked out because when I came to, I saw the pit writhing—moving in waves like the ocean. Not all the people were dead.

I found out that these were the women picked to service the brothel in Auschwitz. This is where my mother had gone. When "used up," the women dug their own graves and were shot.[31]

Block 24, just beside the main gate of Auschwitz, became a brothel. The brothel was in operation until January 1945, and though little is known about the women forced to work here, it is believed they were chosen from non-Jewish inmates. The whole subject is one that most prefer not to talk about, but the suffering endured by these women is perhaps one of the least acknowledged aspects of the history of Auschwitz. (pbs. org/Auschwitz)

For a long time I could not tell this about my mother; I was too ashamed. Finally, I told the people at the United States Holocaust Memorial Museum (USHMM). My daughter, Dahlia, was at the museum, and after I had talked to them, she thought that I was cold because I was shivering. I never told this to my two sons—too degrading. It was better to die by gas than to have this death!

To be fifteen years and to see this after what I had already seen was devastating. I decided that next day I would go to the wire. Why should I stay here? Why should I live? I had no hope.

·· Chapter 10 ··

Harvest

Before I was able to go to the wire, I was selected for a group of 150. I said, "Thank G-d." How I could say that? I don't know. Habit, I guess.

Now you will see how sadistic they were. After they selected us, they took us as if we were going to the crematorium. Inside the building smelled horribly. The big doors leading to the crematorium were open. If you want to know how it feels before death, I can tell you. I said the prayer we say before death. They then marched us out another door. However, before we left the building, I saw the inside of the crematorium.

They took us to cattle trains. I found out they were taking us to farms. I already was in paradise. This was the day that I was supposed to touch the wire, yet I was alive. They brought us to a place where six prisoners of war (POWs) were being held to do forced labor—two Australians, two Scots, and two British.[32]

When we arrived, the SS told the farm manager that we were to be treated differently from the POWS. They said, "Here are the rules: they have to wash but they can not have any soap or towels; you should give them old rags to dry on. They are not allowed in the house. They can have only one blanket—no more. They should be given the leftovers from the family, only the leftovers. If nothing is left, they get nothing."

Eight of us, all girls, were with this particular farmer. We were shoved inside the barn. The hay in a barn needs air so it won't mildew. Therefore, barns have spaces between the boards for air to come through. So it was cold from this air, but we covered ourselves with hay to warm up.

The next morning, the farmer took us out to the field where they were cutting hay. We had to tie the bundles of hay. If we didn't have enough bundles finished, they hit us. The SS were around watching. We worked in pairs, a girl and a POW. For these men the work was not difficult, but we were malnourished, very weak, so for us the work was formidable. The POWs were not allowed to talk to us. When the SS were drinking, the POWs asked us questions: "Who are you?" "Where did you come from?"

Slowly, slowly, we told them the story. They were shocked and surprised. They didn't believe it could be worse than their treatment but they saw us with their own eyes. Then they began to help us when the SS were not looking. They tied the bundles of hay for us.

When there were no leftovers and we were told, "Too bad!" then they stole food for us. They would sneak into the barn and leave us food behind the barn door. We divided this food among ourselves. Unbelievable—such humanity!

They spoke English. We were two years in captivity, so we knew some German. When a person knows German, she can understand some English. The night before they were packing us up to leave, one Englishman wrote to us that he was of the Jewish religion, but he said to destroy the note. He did not want the SS to know. On that day, I decided that there were still Jewish people alive. I felt that I should hope. I should fight. Maybe there is a reason I should live. It was very emotional to find out that one who had helped us was our own. We were not used to this. The next morning we left the farm.

Chapter 11

"Paradise" to Hell

We went from "paradise" to hell. They took us to Stutthof Concentration Camp near Danzig, present day Poland, where there was a typhus epidemic. When they opened the gate, I saw bodies stacked almost as high as houses. The bodies were piled criss-cross. We asked, "What is this?" They replied, "Typhus. We don't have enough people to dig the graves, but you can help us." So some of us dug graves and some dug ditches—*panzersperre*—so tanks couldn't pass over the trenches.

We were each assigned so many feet of trenches to dig. We would be beaten if we didn't accomplish all they expected us to do. A Polish doctor worked next to me. She helped me dig on my side, so I would have the quota amount dug. One day a young German soldier said to me, "You don't look Jewish." I was naïve, so I said, "No, I am a Jew. My parents and grandparents were Jews." He picked up his rifle, hitting me on my arm and breaking it. The pain was terrible but I couldn't let him see this. After he walked away—the trench was a mile long—the doctor next to me took two sticks and placed them on either side of my arm, binding them with a piece of her dress that she had ripped off. Then she took from her pocket two aspirins and gave them to me. She said, "This is the only chance you have. If you go into the *Krankenbau* [hospital barracks] or if you don't, this may well be the end of you.[33]

I don't know how I dealt with the pain, but the doctor and another woman dug my quota for me. After two weeks, the doctor removed the splint and the bone was healed; however, a piece of bone stuck up. The pain was unbelievable. I was ready to give up, but I didn't. I had gained some feeling back in my fingers. When we finished this work, they took us away, telling us, "When the war is over, you can come back and close up the trenches."

They then took us to a munitions factory.

·· Chapter 12 ··

The Munitions Factory

When we arrived at the munitions factory, an SS officer showed us how to put grenades together. He told us, "If you do not put them together correctly, you will be killed. The SS always found something wrong with the grenades my group had worked on. Then they took two to four people outside and shot them as a lesson to all of us. In this factory, I learned to put both bullets and grenades together. One day the American and Russian airplanes came, and they put us outside. I was with my *Lagerschwester* (camp sister). The planes thinking that we were soldiers dove down and shot at us with machine guns.

After this, I heard my camp sister screaming, "What happened to my leg? What happened to my leg? My foot! My foot!" I looked over; she was holding her foot—detached from her leg.

When the airplanes left, they brought us back inside. The ones who were wounded, the ones without arms and legs and feet, they finished off. I don't know how. They left the dead outside. Then I heard more machine gun fire and bombings. We were deep inside Germany. I heard that the factory was closing because the Allies were nearby.

This is when our death march began.

⚥ · Chapter 13 · ⚥

Icicles and Lice

We began the death march with 3000 girls.[34] I ran with rags tied around my feet. It was so cold that icicles were hanging from my hair. During the march, we were kicked to move us on faster or killed if we didn't keep up.

We did not march through cities. We went roundabout in fields. If we were lucky, we found turnips or rotten potatoes in these fields. I had two new *Lagerschwesters*. (If one camp sister died, we chose others.) One day I bent down to pick a vegetable and was hit over the head. My head hurt and I felt as if everything was spinning. I wanted to sit down; however, my sisters said I had to go on because if I didn't the SS would kill me. They told me, "The Americans and Soviets are coming. It won't be much longer and Germany will be defeated."

We walked a day and a half. We passed through one town. They said, "Who are you? Who are you? You don't look like humans." But none of them brought us even one drop of water. So we ate the snow that was on the ground. We also ate potatoes thrown away by the soldiers.

Slowly, slowly, many on the death march were killed. They didn't use bullets on those prisoners who couldn't keep up. There was a way that they could kill them with their rifle butts on the back of their heads. That is how they killed many of us.

One day we came to a small town on a little mountain. We arrived at a huge, huge barn. They were drying hay there. In the middle of the barn was a chemical pool where they loosened paint. We were lying in the hay, which was good because they had been pushing us to walk faster, and we were exhausted.

Lying with us was typhus.[35] So many lice. Dirt and lice equals typhus.

I was lying in the hay. I remember that snow was falling on my chest. I tried to wash myself, to refresh myself. Three girls from my hometown were lying close by. They were very ill. If the Nazis saw that we were ill, they threw us in the chemical pool. Jenny, lying next to me, was found ill. Four people took her body: two took her arms, two her feet; her head was lolling over. She looked at me with a smile. Later I realized that she smiled because for her it was over. Then I heard a splash.

I saw the same thing happen with the other two. Then one day I realized that I would be next. I felt very peaceful. I thought, "How terrific! I, too, am dying. Everything will be just black—no more pain; no more feeling."

Then something happened—the soldiers ran away. The ones, who were still well, looked around for them. No German soldiers! Because the Soviets had arrived! Then the Soviets found us. After they saw us, they sent a message to the nearby city, Kedzierzyn. They had people from there bring horses and wagons and load the bodies and the half dead. I was one of those barely breathing. I was put into one of the many, many wagons.

ᘒ· Chapter 14 ·ᘒ

A White Heaven

I awoke in a totally white room, a crucifix on the wall over my head, with three nuns in white habits hovering. The air around me was clean and calm. The Soviet soldiers had transferred me to the nuns at St. Mary's Hospital. I thought I had died and been put in a non-Jewish heaven. After what I had gone through! I screamed! Immediately a nun turned from her work and reassured her, "You are not dead—you are alive, my child. We will take care of you." I was so badly infested with lice that just to touch any part of my body meant coming away with a handful of lice. I screamed again! "No! No! They have made a mistake! I am not Sara. Sara died. How could she have survived? I'm someone else; I am Maria." For a while this is what I believed.

Except for my frostbitten toes, I discovered that I could feel my body and could move. Despite appeals from the nuns, I felt compelled to leave the hospital to find someone who would know me. I wanted someone else to validate that I was Sara. Otherwise, Sara Kafmonova existed only in a dream back in that barn where the Soviets found her. I sneaked out. I could not trust. I was afraid the nuns would send me back to the concentration camps.

Concentration camp survivors had gathered in the center of Kedzierzyn, dying of typhus and from the effects of rich food eaten too quickly. Many citizens of Kedzierzyn, fearful of the Soviet soldiers, had fled, those remaining lacked compassion for the survivors, so they threw the dead into huge pits. Survivors languished near the pit awaiting their own deaths.

I learned that the soldiers had taken twenty-five girls that they had rescued from the barn to abandoned homes. I was determined to find them. However, my feet had been frostbitten so I couldn't walk. I moved around on all fours or on my behind, desperate to find someone I knew. Because I was like a skeleton with no flesh on my behind and had only tatters for clothing, nothing that would protect me from the ground, I developed sores.

I came to a row of houses. I crawled up three steps to one of them. Inside the house was dark, damp, and cold. Across the room in two small beds were two girls that I recognized, Edith and Chavie, two sisters from Krivé; they were dying. I could hear their cries of misery. They cried for water and food. The Soviets had given them bacon and they had developed diarrhea. I knew if I could find caraway (kimmel) seeds, I could boil these in some water and that would stop the diarrhea. Grandmother Rivka had used a caraway soup to cure stomach ache. I crawled to another abandoned house and found a brown paper bag of caraway seeds and old, hard bread. I also found there a bucket. I crawled to the water and got a bucketful. By this time my knees were raw and bleeding. I needed wood for the fire, so I broke up the children's toys—a cradle and a table and chair set—and made the fire, using pages from some German books to start the fire. When I started to blow on the fire, I coughed blood. Then I cooked a caraway soup. I gave them only this soup. Even after the third day they could not yet eat bread. After eight days they were better. The Russian doctors had told us to start slowly. We hadn't known what would happen if we ate too much or too fast.

Several other concentration camp girls came to stay with us. Whoever could walk went out in search of supplies; in the cupboards and trunks in abandoned houses they found stale bread, a bit of flour, beans, or a potato. Whatever was found was brought back to their communal home and shared with the others.

After three of four weeks the Soviet soldiers called a meeting. Trains to the cities were to begin departing from Kedzierzyn. The Russians announced that relief supplies were being organized by the Red Cross and the Joint Distribution Committee (Joint or JDC).[36] The soldiers offered to carry the girls to the train station in horse drawn wagon.

The girls told me, "We'll be okay. We want to go home to Czechoslovakia. You should try to go home." I decided to go home to see if I could find a relative alive. The trains brought us to Germany, and the trains would take us out of Germany. I crawled and came to one of the trains; I left without the other two. Only Jews traveled on the trains. No guards pushed them in and every door remained open. Every one agreed: the doors must remain open. During the journey, people sat in the door openings inhaling the fresh country air and feeling the freedom of spring breezes.

I didn't know there were organizations such as the United Nations Rescue and Rehabilitation Association (UNRRA),[37] the American Joint Distribution Committee (the Joint), and the International Red Cross.[38] The Red Cross fed us. The Russian soldiers also fed us. Red Cross workers and Russian soldiers brought food and water on board. They distributed bread. Bread to the survivor was the most important thing in the world. They also brought C.A.R.E. packages. For the first time, I saw a box of Corn Flakes. When I learned that Corn Flakes were a breakfast cereal, I envisioned Grandmother Rivka, her head covered with a gaily covered shawl, preparing cereal by grinding dough into farfel. Grandmother Rivka belonged to another lifetime.

During the day, from the train, survivors gazed out on a world they thought had ended when their families were murdered. In this world I felt nothing. Except hunger! I opened a small package of cereal and discovered the pleasant crunch. I unwrapped a cube of sugar and suddenly remembered my cousins; as children we used to squeeze drops of lemon juice onto a sugar cube, a special treat. Freshly baked bread was distributed and I alternated a bite of bread with a nibble of the sugar cube. I was careful to save a piece of bread in my pocket for later.

At night there was fear. The Soviets soldiers fed us, but at night they did terrible things as well. Night after night they raped. I heard screams in the middle of the night. They drank and then raped anyone who looked half decent. This happened even on the train. The women were afraid to tell the Red Cross. I weighed only thirty kilograms; they didn't want me.

The train ran slowly, slowly. When the train reached a place where the tracks had been damaged by the war, it was sometimes delayed for days while the tracks were repaired. The delays didn't bother us. On the train I discovered my philosophy for the rest of my life—I was never going to have it as bad as I already had it, so there is no reason to complain. No crematoriums. No beatings. The war was over but I felt no excitement. In the barn I was relieved when I thought I was dying. When I awoke in St. Mary's Hospital, I realized the struggle would continue. Then I thought: "What am I fighting for? My family is gone!"

We arrived at the Slovak border. Up to the train came a group of the Red Cross. I saw a young man whose family I knew—Zvi Prizant, who belonged to Habonim Dror, a Zionist organization. He knew my future husband; they were in Budapest, Hungary, together, organizing false papers and infiltrating the German army. I said to him, "Zvi, don't you recognize me?" He said, "No." Then I thought, "Why would he recognize me? Look at me. See what they did to me!" I felt as if I were nothing. I said again, "You don't recognize me? He said, "Tell me your name." I answered, "I am Sara." He clapped his hands together and said, "What have they done to you?" Tears came to his eyes. He said, "Where are you going?" I said, "I don't know." He said, "The first thing I am going to do is to take you off this train. You are going to come with me. We have a *kibbutz* in Romania where people who survived the Underground are living."[39] He took me off the train—I was still in a cattle car. There were no passenger cars. However, the car was not crowded; indeed, there were not many of us left. Zvi was very emotional and crying. He gave me to a non-Jewish family. He told them, "Fatten her up. I can't send her where I want to send her the way she looks."

Zvi then told me, "You have a second cousin in Romania—Sara Rasmovich. The Underground had sent her to Budapest to hide out." Zvi sent a messenger, for there were no working telegraphs: "I have the first survivor, Sara Kafmanova. Tell Sara Rasmovich that I will send her cousin to Romania as soon as she can travel, in three or four weeks.

I started to eat better. But I coughed a lot. Sometimes I coughed up blood. My broken arm was sore. My feet and toes—if cold, they hurt; if warm, they hurt. But when I was in pain, I would say to myself, "What do you care? You are alive! You were through much worse than this." This is how I talked to myself.

After a number of weeks, I arrived in Bucharest, Romania. The following is Ernest Paul's account of Sara's "Train to Freedom":

The representatives of the various organizations—the anti-fascist community headed by Jacob Smeterer, the Habonim Dror representative, and the Red Cross representatives made a joint appeal to the Romanian, Hungarian, Polish, German, and Czech authorities requesting train transportation from Bucharest, Romania, for survivors of the camps, of the partisans, and of the Warsaw Ghetto, among them children ages fifteen to twenty.

To obtain the coordination of all the authorities was a monumental challenge. After lengthy, intensive efforts, thirteen cars on two freight trains were made available. The freight cars were clean and equipped with bunkbeds, a table in each car, secured to the floor, and a few benches. The doors were on a chain to keep them a bit open during the trip, to give fresh air and to make the passengers feel that the train was not the same as the trains that had taken them to the concentration camps. The second train would depart thirty days after the first. Each train had a doctor and a nurse on board; in charge of the technical crew were Jacob Smeterer, Zvi Prizant, and Shany Lazar and Moshe Lazarovics were in charge of logistics. They represented Habonim Dror. *The train left from Bucharest to the nearest station, to Auschwitz.*

The first train was loaded with the precious cargo—460 children and survivors. They heard the sound of the locomotive and felt the train moving. They burst into tears and singing at the same time "Hatikva" (The Hope), the anthem written by Naphtali Herz Imber in the early 1880s, which looks to the day the Jewish people will one day return to their homeland. "Hatikva" became the national anthem of Israel in 1948. The train traveled from Auschwitz-Birkenau to Prague to Humenne, Slovakia, to Czechoslovakia, Germany, Hungary, and Romania—a long, exhausting trip of twelve days because the tracks were limited, restricted to the scheduled trains. Upon arrival at Kibbutz Maria Rossetti 21 or the Kibbutz Frumka, the receiving committee processed the individuals; others were placed in different preliminary housing.

The second train left Poland thirty days later. The train ride was very emotional; each survivor still had skepticism and concern as to the destination of the train. They wondered: Would the different border authorities respect the permits of the train? Each individual had hope of a new beginning but the final destination was uncertain. Each had hopes and dreams about family members that may have survived.

The morale builders throughout the trips were the Zionist youth movement representatives headed by Zvi Prizant. It took long days and sleepless nights to assure all of the passengers that they were "free"—free to face a new world, a new beginning, and a new life.

Sara, among others, waited for the freedom train to arrive. Sara had decided to get on the train to take her out of the concentration camp environment. As she boarded the train, suddenly Sara recognized a familiar face, a young man from a neighboring town, Chust. Zvi used to come often to Krivé, Sara's town, to spread Zionist ideals and ideologies.

"Zvi! Zvi!" Sara cried out. "Look.   Here I am, Sara Kafmanova from Krivé. Zvi paused and looked around, wondering: Where is this cry coming from? "Who is it," he said. "I am Sara Kafmanova" was the reply. Zvi stared at Sara and recognition finally came to him. He clasped his large gentle hands, swayed, and his eyes fill with tears. "My G-d! What have they done to you?"

Zvi was hungry for any information regarding survivors from Krivé, so Sara told him about Edith and Chavie, who could not come on this train but who would follow on another train. Zvi told her that survivors from Budapest who were hidden in bunkers in the forest were living in a kibbutz *in Bucharest, where people were recuperating.   He told her, "You have there a cousin, whose mother was your mother's favorite aunt. Her name is a Sarah Rasmovich, a survivor from one of the bunkers in Budapest. But, listen, I can't send you there looking like this! First we will have to put some meat on your bones. My G-d, . . . what can you weigh? Seventy pounds? Sara, you are the first of those I knew from before the war that I have seen after the camps."*

I'll bring you to the kibbutz *in Bucharest, but first, you'll stay with a couple, a woman I know in Humenne. They will take care of you.*

So Zvi led Sara off the train and brought her to the house of a Slavic couple, parents of adult children who no longer lived at home. The house was spacious. The family received her with open arms. Sara was given a separate bedroom, and Olga, the woman of the house, was very friendly and caring, looking after her. The first thing she did was bring in a large basket of assorted fresh fruit from their own garden, followed with fresh bread and milk. Sara was surprised to see all this fresh produce. She'd imagined that the world had been destroyed with all this included. The most important subject of conversation between them was food. Olga asked, "What can I cook for you, Sara? Something special?" However, Sara had no appetite because she had lost her taste buds; therefore, she was not very demanding. The fresh fruits and vegetables helped her gradually to increase her appetite for more solid food, such as stuffed cabbage and chicken paprika. She did gain some weight before Zvi returned four weeks later to take her to the train to Bucharest, Romania. However, her hair had not grown much, and she was still coughing up blood and hurting all over physically and emotionally.

On the train she met up with some fellow survivors, who formed a group to share and care for each other. They were all sick; some more than others—some had lost an eye; some, an arm or a leg.

Sara felt rich. Olga had given her a pair of shoes and a couple dresses bundled up in a large scarf. The next day when Sara unbundled the scarf, she found fruits, bread and butter, and a big salami—a pleasant surprise to all. They debated about cutting the salami, but they couldn't resist. They sliced the salami with a knife that Olga had included. The bread, the butter, and the fruits were all shared—they had an enjoyable feast. They had these provisions in addition to some food rations provided by the various agencies.

Although they were on the train among some friendly faces, they were anxious, wondering if the train would really arrive in Bucharest or would it take them back to the concentration camp. Eventually Sara arrived in Bucharest crying with happy tears.

At the Bucharest train station there was a part of a corridor blocked off. In this area were representatives of the Zionist organization, the Hebrew Immigration Aid Society (HIAS), the Joint, and other Jewish organizations. Zvi and his Habonim Dror *companions had identified those that would be taken to* Kibbutz Frumka and Kibbutz Maria Rossetti 21, among them Sara.

Sara Triumphant!

The others were placed in different homes and hotels, awaiting a destination of their choosing. Some returned to their homes, looking to find some family members; others chose different designated refugee camps all over Europe.

⤳ Chapter 15 ⤝

Cared For!

In Bucharest, I was sent to a magnificent villa that had belonged to the Germans who had run away. The address was Maria Rossetti 21. When I arrived, I saw normal people—the first ones that I had seen. My cousin knew that I was coming. We were the only ones left of our family. She saw me and started screaming, "Sara." I, too, was screaming, "Sara." Ernest (Janchi Pa'l)—one of the men in charge of the *kibbutz*—saw and heard us. My cousin had been hit on the head and was acting a little strangely; therefore, when Ernest heard us both yelling "Sara," he thought that he would have two crazy Saras to look after. He thought we were both nuts.

Two hundred people were living in this *kibbutz*. They came to look at me as if I were a freak or an alien. They asked me if I knew their family members. I explained that in the concentration camps, we did not have names, only numbers.

I was so sick that I needed a lot of help. Ernest called a meeting. He said, "We need three girls to help: one to wash, one to dress, and one to cook for Sara. One of you needs to keep her company. You have to ask her what she wants to eat." These three girls helped me.

Eva, the wife of Zvi, who had pulled me off the train, helped me and became my best friend. They took care of my arm. I was still coughing; I had pneumonia, so the doctor gave me aspirin.

Before Zvi found me at the train station, I had said to myself, "I don't want to be Sara. I don't want a Jewish name. I will be Maria." After a while I said to myself, "How can a Sara be a Maria? I have to be a Sara and be a very good Sara to make up for the ones who are no longer here."

Ernest remembers Sara's arrival at the *kibbutz* in Bucharest:

Sara walked in through the iron gate of the kibbutz *with Zvi. A welcome committee (all of us) waited anxiously. Suddenly we heard a shriek, a cry of "Sara." "Sara." Both Saras ran to each other while continuing to scream "Sara." "Sara." The arriving Sara and Sara, the cousin who was already a member of the* kibbutz, *met. For a moment we thought we were witnessing a tragic mental breakdown.*

We eventually realized what was happening and quickly began helping and embracing the Sara that had just arrived. I supported Sara on one side, helping her walk up the wide stairs, while her cousin, Sara Rasmovich, supported her on the other side. We went into a small peaceful room where five other girls were living.

As a member of the mazkirut *(management), I initiated a meeting with Zvi, the head of the* kibbutz *and others. Sara looked sick and frail. We decided to make her cousin Sara, and Zvi's* chavara, *Eva, available to help Sara to recuperate. They were very helpful—Eva remained a lifetime friend of Sara and me.*

Sara had many visitors, well wishers offering help. Some came to seek information about their loved ones in concentration camps, "Do you by chance know my sister, Mirel?" "Maybe you met my mother Shuszi Greenberg, blue eyes like mine?"

Sara was comfortable in her bed; however, she developed a fever and coughed up blood. The girls fed her and bathed her as she recounted her experiences—and nightmares. In the communal kitchen Eva and her cousin Sara prepared special

food for her, but she had no appetite. Eva would insist, "Just a few more bites."
"Tell us, Sara. What would you really like to eat? Whatever you want, just tell
us." Momentarily piqued by the question, Sara replied: "Scrambled eggs and a
sour pickle." Everyone was surprised by this special order.

At that moment I entered the room. Although I was only seventeen, I
radiated a quiet, capable strength, and my blue eyes reflected serious determination,
determination not only for my own survival but also for the survival of our people.
I was determined to realize our collective dream of a Jewish homeland. I had
for three years outwitted and outlasted the Nazis. But for now my attention was
focused on Sara.

Eva informed me that Sara would eat eggs and pickles. I knelt beside
Sara's bed, "Eggs and sour pickles? I'll go all over Bucharest until I find them
somewhere." I jumped on my battered motorcycle. Eggs and a pickle was the
most urgent mission of the day. Sure enough, later Eva brought Sara a plate of
warm scrambled eggs. The eggs were fresh, laid that dawn in some farmer's hen
loft, and the sour pickle, thinly sliced, was from a deli. In my mind a commitment
was born; I knew that no other task was more important than feeding Sara. Eva
and her cousin Sara also were committed to the task.

Our days on the kibbutz *were structured and full of hope, for we shared*
a common goal, to make aliyah *to reach the Promised Land which awaited its*
ingathering of souls yearning for renewal. Zvi taught classes in Hebrew and
about the realities of life in Palestine. Teachers arrived from Palestine to instruct
us in the agricultural demands of the desert. They also prepared the survivors for
real kibbutz *life, which in the Holy Land promised to be harsh and demanding*
amid hostile Arab neighbors.

We learned the songs and dances of hope with young people who had avoided
concentration camps by enduring underground existences in bunkers.

Each week the Joint (JDC) posted long lists of names and addresses of
American Jews who were searching for European relatives, and a few people were
reunited, but Sara had no American relatives.

Cousin Sara Rasmovich spent hours at her bedside and slowly Cousin Sara revealed her story:

Sara, Rasmovich's family had lived about two hours northeast of Krivé. Sara had attended boarding school in Budapest, so initially chance had saved her from deportation to the ghetto. Later on there was a teacher who helped her acquire false papers and these papers protected her for a while. She told me that one day the soldiers come marching with their boots and their guns into her school, and she was frightened. One soldier took out a piece of paper and read off her name right there in her history class. Someone had betrayed her, someone she knew and probably smiled and spoke to. Ach!

Then Sara explained that she and Janchi (Ernest) had known each other well in Budapest as members of Habonim, the Zionist youth organization:

Sara you should know, I owe my life to Janchi. He took me to a bunker: one day he ran into me and told me that my Hungarian accent could cost me my life. He told me that it was becoming more and more dangerous outside and that I should go into hiding. I agreed and jumped on his motorcycle. Forty five minutes later we arrived at the bunker.

The bunkers were underground rooms, just large enough to accommodate sleeping space on tiered planks. Evenings, well past sunset, one at a time and always with one standing guard, the young people would venture up through the camouflaged trap door and spent a few anxiety-laden moments inhaling fresh air. All the other hours of the day they remained as motionless as possible.

In the bunkers we experienced all the fear and uneasiness natural to human beings forced to endure this existence. Our imaginations were quickened. Our bodies in the dank darkness were besieged by crawling things whose territory we were sharing. We felt every discomfort one can imagine. Ernest was our provider, our dependable link to the world outside.

These desperate arrangements, however, entailed the very real danger of betrayal, for it often came to pass that those hidden in the blackness of a bunker would hear the ominous sounds of the approaching boot steps of Hungarian police, pounding on the floor boards directly above our heads. Then the trap door would lift.

Early morning the Hungarian Nazi forces were led to the bunker by one of our own who was arrested previously. He was not able to withstand the pain inflicted on him during the investigations.

There was no way we could resist the twelve police— well armed with gas bombs, grenades, and automatic weapons—who surrounded the bunker. Twenty two of us were arrested and taken to the Margit Körút Military Prison for investigation (subsequently we were rescued by our underground).

Ernest saved my life by insisting that I seek safety with the Underground forces in Budapest, Hungary. I am indebted to him forever, Sara.

Chapter 16

Gladiolas

Ernest Pa'l (Janchi), one of the leaders of the *kibbutz*, took care of me, and we became close. One day I said, "I would like some sour pickles and an egg." Ernest went out on his motorcycle to get these for me. He was very kind and caring.

Soon Ernest told me that he had to go back to Budapest. He had to leave to care for orphaned Jewish children.[40] He wanted me to go with him. This created a dilemma because I was only sixteen. I couldn't travel with a man unless I was married. Who would want to marry me? Outside I was nothing—no hair. I looked terrible. Ernest saw more of what was inside. He saw more than I saw. He said, "Why not marry me?" I said, "I can't do that. If I stay alive, I need an education." I didn't want to marry Ernest, but my cousin, Sara Rasmovich, warned me, "If you are not going to marry Janchi, I will marry him." I loved him, so I married him. We married on July 13, 1945.

No rabbis. No priests. Zvi was the "captain." He married us. We had two bottles of wine, some bottles of water, and gladiolas on the table.

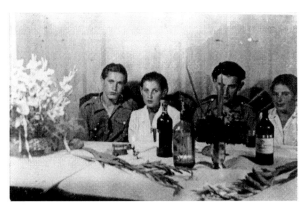

Bucharest, Romania, July 14, 1945, Sara and Ernest's Wedding:
L to R Ernest, Sara, Willi, Shoshana

In 2009, Ernest wrote his account of Sara's arrival at the kibbutz and their marriage:

Sara was sixteen years old when she arrived to the kibbutz *in Bucharest. She could hardly walk. She looked like a skeleton. She had no hair; she had lost her hair during the typhus epidemic in the concentration camp. During the first days and weeks our mission was to get her well as quickly as possible.*

However, I saw much more than her physical appearance.

She drew my attention with her shining brown eyes and more so with her sense of humor and her strength in facing a new life. It did not take too long for us to get to know each other, as I was at her bedside quite often as she was recuperating. As spring came around in early April she had mildly recuperated, so I took her for short walks outside. As the sun shone, her face reflected a warmth and affection.

One beautiful morning I saw a young woman. Her body had become stronger. Her hair had started to grow back. Her beautiful face and smile strongly captured my attention. My heart dictated a further special relationship.

We lived in the kibbutz *under the same roof. Because we had no parents and Sara was sixteen, I, at seventeen years old, introduced the subject of her becoming my* chavara, *my friend, which meant eating together, dancing together, and singing together. At first conversation she was cool to my idea. It took a lot more conversation until Sara admitted her "special feelings" for me.*

Everyone in the kibbutz and particularly her cousin Sara told her that we were a couple from heaven (himmel—angels). We loved each other; our love grew stronger every day.

We decided we would get married, so we had our meeting with the head of the kibbutz—the "captain": Zvi. We shared with him our plans for marriage. Zvi was happy for both of us. Because we had no rabbi on the kibbutz, Zvi stated that he would marry us as "captain of the ship."[41] After all, he was in charge. "As a matter of fact," Zvi said, "another couple in the kibbutz, Shoshana and Willi Braunstein, your good friends, have also announced to him their decision to marry."

Plans were discussed. Zvi stated, "We have a limited budget; therefore, we must make the weddings economically affordable. It is two couples, two bottles of wine at the head of the table, and we will bring in an accordion player. We also have a good friend in the kibbutz named Lacy who plays the guitar. Both grooms will get blue shirts (Chulza Tnua—Youth Movement "uniform" shirt with two pockets), and the brides will be given white shirts.

The simchah (joyous celebration) started slowly at 7:00 PM and went on until 7:00 in the morning. Two hundred members of the kibbutz, our friends, celebrated by singing and dancing all night.

This was the first wedding in the kibbutz that had a special meaning to all of us—reflecting new life and new hope for the future.

When we were eventually immigrated to Palestine (pre Israel) and were living there, Sara became pregnant with our first child, Dahlia. Sara said to me, "We are not even legally married."

I promised Sara, "One day I will get a rabbi and we will be officially married."

·· Chapter 17 ··

Love's Miracle

We stayed six weeks in Budapest caring for the orphan children. First there were twenty-two but the number grew to sixty. After the six weeks, the Jewish Agency hired professionals to manage the orphanage and care for the children.

Ernest and I then traveled to southern Italy to *Frumka Kibbutz* at Port Tricasa, where other survivors had found refuge. One night I had a high temperature. Ernest took me to the doctor. The doctor said that the four lobes of my lungs were affected by tuberculosis.[42] He said, furthermore, that I needed to be in a sanatorium because I was contagious with open tuberculosis. Because Ernest had contacts among the Jewish agencies, he arranged for me to be admitted into a special hospital in Rome, the Carlo Forlanini Hospital.[43]

I was seventeen years old and underage, so I was not allowed out unless I had permission. I asked to speak to the Mother Superior. She told the others, "Let her out whenever she wants out. She is not seventeen or eighteen. She is sixty or seventy years old. She is very wise after what she went through. Let her visit her friends."

My husband didn't give up. He came everyday to see me. I didn't get better. Ernest went on a rampage. "She is not improving! What are our options? The doctors told us about another "healing home," a famous sanatorium, in the mountains bordering Switzerland—Merano.[44] He took me there because I was very ill. I was losing the weight that I had just gained.

In Merano, at first I didn't get any better. The doctors told Ernest, "There is no hope. Leave her here. You are a young man. Even if she does survive, she can't have children." Ernest replied, "I don't care. There are plenty of children who need parents. We will adopt. She is all that I want. I will be here as long as she has a breath of air."

I gradually was cured and released from the sanatorium at Merano.

I began to regain my appetite. Ernest took me on a train with a sleeping car. Near Milano, I said, "Dov, I feel like eating a roll." Really! He bought me a roll with butter.

We came to a little city close to Rome—about an hour away, to the *Kibbutz Ladisipoly*. I began to thrive. Within three months my hair grew in.

Merano, Italy, 1946:
Sara, third from left, with nurses and friends

I grew inches. I gained weight. I swam out to the fishermen and swam back—like a fish. People didn't believe their eyes. I had become a pretty girl. I felt good. I only had to go to the doctors for checkups.

In the Italian *kibbutz*, I did my job. We were preparing to go to Israel. My husband was a Zionist and wanted to make *aliyah* to Israel.[45] However, I didn't want to live on a kibbutz in Israel and be closed in again. I didn't tell him this, however.

Milano, Italy, 1947:
Sara at the Piazza Duomo

Ernest wrote his account of their journey
to Hungary, Italy, and Israel:
"The Long Journey to Eretz Yisrael":

Milano, Italy, 1947:
Sara and Ernest

*Soon after we were married in Bucharest, I was given orders to go back
to Budapest, Hungary. While there, Sara and I received a new assignment from
the leader of our organization,* Dror Habonim, *to manage and supervise an
orphanage home of twenty-five children, ages two to four. Some of these children
had been abandoned by their one surviving parent. The single parent could not
longer support the child or children. Sara had great satisfaction when given the
opportunity to help others, particularly children.*

*Gradually, the number of children grew to over sixty. Our attachment to the
children grew stronger every day. The hard work and the responsibility were most
rewarding to both of us. The love of the children made it all easy and worthwhile.
However, after three months a professional team was hired by Jewish agencies to
relieve us.*

*We continued our journey. We had new orders to take a group of thirty-four
young survivors to Italy to get them on a ship to* Eretz Yisrael.

*Our first stop in Italy was Trieste. Then we went on Milano via Unione 5,
which was the headquarters of the Jewish agencies. This was a stop-over where we
awaited further instructions. The Jewish brigade of the British Army took charge*

of all activities; they worked tirelessly to provide us with temporary shelter, food, clothing, and medicine.

The brigade commander Meier Swartz, a colonel from Kibbutz Ein-Charod, *and the head of the Jewish agencies, Mayer Rabinovich, were the contact and the negotiators with the Italian government to legitimatize our stay in Italy and our moving around throughout the country while waiting for a ship to make sail to* Eretz Yisrael *(Pre-Israel).*

After a short stay in the north of Italy a group of our Frumka Kibbutz *members from Bucharest arrived led by Zvi Prizant and Eva. It was a great reunion. A month later we were given instructions to travel to the very south of Italy, a beautiful small fisherman village south of Bari, Tricasa Port. The villa had previously been occupied by the Nazi regional headquarters. The villa was vacant, waiting for our arrival. This house was named* Kibbutz Frumka *(the same as in Bucharest) because most of us were transferred from Bucharest. The Italian population embraced us, offering all assistance possible. Because this was after the war and there were shortages, they did not have much to give; however, their friendship was greatly appreciated by all of us. We raised a Jewish and Italian flag on the poles where the Italian Fascist Mussolini and Nazi Germany flags once flew.*

Arriving at Tricasa, for the first time in our lives, we saw trees full of fresh smelling, tasty fruits: oranges and tangerines. The poor Italian families gladly shared their fruits in their gardens with the survivors.

The kibbutz *became a training school to prepare us to better understand the challenges that would face us in* Eretz Yisrael.

Lecturers from the Jewish Brigade were frequent visitors, as well as Shlichim (Hebrew for emissary) from kibbutzim in Eretz Yisrael. *All members in the kibbutz were eager to learn not only our future language but also all aspects of life in* Eretz Yisrael.

Sara was still sick, so the local doctors that we visited tried to treat her active tuberculosis with penicillin that we were able to obtain through the Jewish agencies. We stayed for six months in Tricasa Port, but Sara was not getting better. On the contrary, she was worse. The Italian doctors told us about a well known hospital in Rome specializing in the healing of tuberculosis. They urged me to get her to this institution, Carlo Forlanini, as soon as possible.

Therefore, I made contact in Rome with our headquarters and the head of the Jewish agency, Mayer Rabinovich, presenting to him medical evidence of Sara's condition and asking him to save her life. I asked him to contact the hospital, asking them to accept Sara with no insurance and no money. Rabinovich was referred to the health authorities of the City of Rome, who considered the medical evidence that Sara would infect others and could die in less than six months unless our request was approved.

I took Sara on the first train Evailable to Rome. Upon our arrival we first went to the headquarters of the Jewish agency, where we were provided with all necessary documents for Sara's immediate admission into the hospital.

Carlo Forlanini Hospital was a clean, spectacular hospital that occupied a large park, four square blocks, on the outskirts of Rome. The beautiful garden with blooming trees and flowers, the walkway between the trees, and the fresh air— all these surroundings made us feel welcomed.

Carlo Forlanini was not only a hospital it was a sanatorium, a healing center. We were full of hope that this would be the place where Sara would get well. The staff and doctors were extremely friendly. I was allowed to stay in the hospital overnight with Sara. Their examination started the following morning. The examination confirmed the seriousness of the illness that Sara was suffering. The doctors predicted a minimum required stay of six to twelve months.

As Sara was getting treatments she was told about another new person, also a concentration camp survivor. This survivor was Bumi Prizant, Zvi's younger brother. Sara was happy to meet someone who spoke the same languages, Yiddish and Hungarian, because her Italian was very new.

Because they were not bed-bound, they took daily walks in the facilities. These walks were a part of the healing process. Unfortunately, four months later Bumi Prizant died. He was only seventeen years old, handsome and smart, hoping to live to reunite with his brother, *Zvi*, and to make aliyah *to* Eretz Yisrael. *Bumi died after catching a minor cold. This was devastating to the family and particularly to Sara. In a way she saw in Bumi a reflection of her own misery—a friend with the same illness, the same hopes and dreams, the same aspirations to live and to see the light at the end of their hospitalization.*

As Bumi's life light was extinguished, Sara broke down in my arms, crying, "My chances, my destiny are the same. I will never make it out of here. After all my lungs, my tuberculosis, is worst than Bumi's was."

Gathering all my strength I repeatedly tried to reassure her, "Your case is different. I love you. I need you. You will get well."

But Sara lost her smile, the luster in her eyes, and her will to live. It was not until I solicited the help of her medical doctor, who ordered psychological treatment, that she made progress after weeks of treatments.

During this time, my assignment was at the headquarters of the Jewish agency as a liaison between Dror Habonin movement and Jewish agency. Among other responsibilities, my job was as a contact for other young survivors coming through Rome daily. Being in Rome I could visit Sara often.

My favorite time was our walks. Our talks were a contributing factor to her healing. I was helping with her progress, visiting her every day.

During the next three months, Sara started to feel better; she made many friends and learned the Italian language. Sara loved some of the Italian weekly magazines. These kept her company during the long, lonely hours, days, and nights.

I came to visit her daily. I began to see her beauty grow. I saw her long brown hair that grew longer every day. Her deep brown eyes had a glimmer of hope. I could see strength and confidence in her beautiful posture. The environment at the hospital, the gardens, the air, the trees, helped her to make the best of a difficult reality. She definitely fit in with the beautiful Italian women. However, as time went on my patience grew thin. I requested a meeting with her medical team. Psychologically she was handling her situation better. But medically was the problem. The doctors told me her tuberculosis was still too active.

They said that by now they had expected more progress.

As to my persistence question, "What can be done to improve her healing process?" The doctors asked me to leave the room, so they could discuss the options amongst themselves. The reply I was given was that Sara would need to be transferred to another institution—Merano—high in the Italian Swiss Alps Mountains in the Northern part of Italy.

They told me, "Merano is the world's most famous sanitarium and Sara needs to be transferred there as soon as possible." The doctors offered to help with the transfer because Sara was one of their favorite patients. They said, "She has suffered enough. We will do everything it takes, and on your part you have to do the same."

I thanked the doctors. I sat with Sara for hours as I saw her tears, her anxiety, and her disappointment overwhelming her.

I took a few deep breaths wiping away her tears and mine. I told her, "I am stronger; you can depend on me. I love you more than you can imagine. I will get you to Merano, and you will recover. You must trust me and believe me, Sara." She broke down crying. I stood near her as a strong pillar that she could lean on.

I contacted my superiors at the Jewish agency. I shared with them our situation as to Sara's failing health. They embraced me and promised to do everything necessary to get her to Merano.

Their joint effort with the doctors from Carlo Forlanini resulted in receiving the approval necessary to move Sara. It took fourteen long days. From the Jewish Agency I received money for train tickets and accommodations in order to stay with Sara for one week.

The trip from Rome to Merano through Milano and Geneva took almost two days. A special chain train took us from downtown Merano to the top of the highest mountain bordering Italy and Switzerland. At the top of the mountain was the sanitarium. This was my last hope for Sara to recuperate. We were in the midst of magnificent Italian Swiss architecture, lush thick forests, and flower gardens. Above all was the warm greeting from the admitting staff.

I said to her, "Look at this place, Sara. This is all for you." Sara began wiping away her tears.

As we toured the facilities I constantly and repeatedly reassured her: "You will be coming home from here healthy, you will see. You must believe. You must have confidence; you are in good hands."

As she settled into a room with clean spaces and big open windows to the garden and flowers, basking in the bright warm sunshine, she calmed down. I saw a glimmer of hope in her face.

At the meeting with the medical staff after they had finished evaluating her portfolio, we were advised that her recovery time would be approximately one year. "Don't be concerned, mia bambino (my child)," one of the doctors consoled her in his attempt to lift Sara's spirit and hopes. "After all, you are in the best place in the world. We need you to be strong and positive. We will need your help because confidence and will power are all part of the healing process."

As we settled into the room, we looked at each other, hugging, kissing, and crying. I told her, "Sara, I love you. I will do everything I can, even if I have to go back to work in Rome." Numerous letters were exchanged between us, almost daily. Every month I visited Sara. She seemed to be thriving in this new, friendly environment with the wonderful medical care. I told her, "The special air, the good doctors, and most important your positive attitude will get you well."

It took nine months of healing, months that saved her life. During my ninth visit I was overwhelmed, pleasantly surprised, because her doctors told me that Sara was healthy and ready to go home. They said, "The tuberculosis is healed. It is non active; however, Sara, you need to take care. Do not smoke. Do not drink alcohol excessively (she never smoked nor drank alcohol, so this was a no brainer). Eat good and dress well to avoid catching a cold. Most of all, enjoy life!

"Arrivederci, bellissima," (Goodbye, beautiful one), the doctors wished us warmly, "Farewell, good luck, and a good life."

We left the hospital and decided to spend two days in a beautiful small villa, Hotel Casel in the city. This was our first opportunity to visit the famous city of

Merano. The two days and nights became our most remembered happy days.

"We are together again. I will never let you out of my sight," I whispered in her ears. "We have survived another hurdle in our life."

I purchased two tickets to Rome. When we arrived, our friends and colleagues were waiting for us to congratulate Sara on her recovery.

Sara and I were then sent to Kibbutz *Ladisipoly, a one hour trolley ride from Rome. This was a tourist resort with one of the many beautiful beaches on the Mediterranean Sea. The* kibbutz *was already established with over 150 survivors waiting for their aliyah to* Eretz Yisrael. *Sara thrived in the fresh sea air.*

While we were there, I became aware that my brother Emil, a survivor of a Nazi concentration camp was living in a DP camp in Germany. I managed to contact him through the Joint (see note 37). I invited and urged him to join me. Two weeks later we were reunited in the kibbutz. *There he met Lili and they married. They as well tried to immigrate to Palestine but were captured by the British and sent to Cyprus where their first child, Rifka, was born. They were detained there for eleven months before joining us in Palestine.*

Chapter 18

Emigration

If we had gone to Palestine illegally, Britain would have sent us to Cyprus. Ernest arranged false papers that stated we were Palestinian-born. We were nearly there, when Ernest asked me, "Honey, which *kibbutz* do you want to go on?" I said, "I don't want to go on a *kibbutz*." He said, "What do you mean? We talked all those times." I said, "You talked all those times. If you remember while you talked all those times, I kept quiet. Ernest, I cannot live in a *kibbutz*, in a regimented life. I have to be free to come and go."

There again, I feel, he gave up his dreams for me.

We arrived in Haifa.[46] We lived in a small hotel for ten days. Then we were transferred to a refugee camp near Haifa—Bat Galim.

When the U.N. voted on Israel, Ernest found a hotel room in Haifa where we waited with many others for the last vote. On May 14, 1948, independence was declared.[47]

Israel, 1948: Sara and Ernest
(in military uniform)

Then we sang and danced the Hora with thousands of others that spontaneously poured out into the street.

However, it wasn't a month before Ernest was called into the army.

Women, too, were called up, but not me because of the TB. I lived in a one room apartment. This was heaven. Anything was better than the shelters I had had during the war. I had a skill because of my previous work in an ammunition factory, so I could help with the war effort. I volunteered to work in munitions. Every day they took me to a secret place. Ernest's sister, Chaja, went with me. She had made bullets before. I checked my work carefully. These were for my people. Even at night I thought, "Did I do it right?" I was scrupulous.

Every three months, they would check my lungs. I was better and better; I continued to improve. One day the lung specialist said, "Go home and have a baby." I went home and told Ernest. He didn't believe me because he knew that I badly wanted to have a baby. He went and talked with the doctor. The doctor

said, "Sara is young. She is completely healed. She can have a baby."

It didn't take long for me to get pregnant with my daughter, Dahlia, born on July 13, 1949. What did I say? I prayed, "You have taken away but you have also given to me." It was a miracle.

Tivon, Israel, 1947
Sara's Identity card

Soon after, Stewart (Shlomu), little "Ben Gurion," as they called him, was born on March 17, 1954. My husband was in politics by then.

For his *bris*, they closed down the office of the *Histarut* in Haifa. The Minister of Labor, Josef Almogi, was Sewart's godfather. We had the *bris* in a huge tent gifted to Israel by King Abdullah I of Jordan (1946-1951). So I had two miracles—Dahlia and Stewart.

My husband worked, and we both went to evening school and raised our children. In the meantime, Ernest was invited by his brother, Ville, to visit him in the United States. My husband went for a visit

Israel, 1951: Sara

Tivon, Israel: Sara and Dahlia, three years old, 1954

and I stayed in Israel. After awhile my brother-in-law, Villi invited me to the U.S. as well. Ernest wanted me to come for a vacation, to enjoy life. I joined him in the U.S., the golden land of opportunity. I told Ernest, "I would really like to live here. The U.S. is a free country. I could give my kids everything. Life in Israel is difficult." Ernest didn't complain, but he was never for it. We stayed a year. I had a store. I learned the language. My children went to school—Stewart to nursery school; Dalia to kindergarten. But Ernest wanted to go back to Israel, and he did in 1956. I returned six months later with the children.

Ernest relates his story of their emigration from Italy:

Considering Sara's past and my activities in the Jewish agency and Habonim Dror, *the directors decided to give us special treatment. We were provided newly produced "false" documents, train tickets from Roma to Napoli, and two tickets on an Italian passenger ship, Napoly-Haifa. The documents were based on the fact that each of us had arrived in Italy before the war, with our Palestinian parents, but had become separated from them, so after our marriage, we were returning home to Palestine.*

As I was too young to be married, it was decided to alter my birth year from 1928 to 1926 to avoid the suspicion of the British authorities. They strictly controlled immigrants' arrivals in Haifa. This method of aliyah *was used selectively by the Jewish agency; this was known as* aliyah-gimel. *Most others made illegal* aliyah *on vessels contracted from Italian, Spanish, and Greek ship owners. Most of the vessels were cargo or fishing vessels converted to carry passengers; the lower deck was transformed to three or four level bunk beds with very limited space between the beds to maximize the capacity. Many thousands wound up in Cyprus, as Emil, my brother, and Lili, his wife, did, when the British authorities restricted entry to Palestine. This was* aliyah bet.

Other methods of aliyah *were for those that had close relatives living in Palestine. They were able to get official entry as part of unifying families. This was* aliyah alev.

Our ship, the passenger ship, Napoly-Haifa, was by no means a luxury ship; however, for us, the first time in our life on a ship was a luxury. Approximately 200 passengers and twenty-five or thirty crew members were on this relatively small ship.

Meals were served three times daily in a clean dining room; the food and service were good and plentiful.

The journey to Haifa, Israel, took us fourteen days—ten rough days. The ocean was inconsiderate with the Jewish passengers; the waves were high as we had strong winds. Each wave lifted the vessel and tossed us from side to side indiscriminately. Sara held on to me for dear life. These waves did not agree with her; therefore, she was seasick for ten out of the fourteen days. I did not get sick, so I was holding on to Sara because she was constantly vomiting. Many of the passengers kept company with Sara, for they experienced the same sickness as did some crew members.

When we arrived at Haifa two representatives from the Jewish agency, an immigration authority representative from Haganah *defense forces, and a representative of* Habonim Dror *came on board the ship. They called our names; we were the first two passengers off the ship.*

As we waited for our luggage, two medium size soft suitcases, we were briefed by the Haganah *representatives about the Arab unrest and the struggle for an independent Jewish state that was well on its way.*

The Habonim Dror *representative was Yischak Pundek from* Kibbutz *Alonim (near Tivon). He and I had met in Italy while he was in the British-Jewish brigade. Yischak invited us to join his* kibbutz. *Sara quietly said, "I am very tired. I cannot go any place now; I need to rest." The journey on the ship had taken a hard toll on Sara. Her tired, pale face reflected her condition. So the decision was made by our resident receiving committee to put us into a small hotel on the Hadar Hacarmel on Herzl Street.*

The city of Haifa has three tiers. In those days they were described as follows:

A.   The Har-HaCarmel-Achuza Neve Sha'anan: *the mountain sides of the city had a 99% Jewish population.*

B.   Hadar HaCarmel: *the middle level of the city: mostly populated by Jewish families (approximately 95%).*

C.   Hair Hatachtit: *the lower level of the city spreading to the sea, including the first major trading port of Israel; this part was populated with a majority of Arab families and restaurants.*

Very soon after our arrival the Arabs began an intifada, *a rebellion or uprising, to fight the Jewish population with all means; their leaders promised them liberation. They were also promised that if they captured and destroyed the*

Tivon, Israel, 1952:
Ernest and Sara

Jewish families, they would be awarded with the properties and businesses of the Jews.

*The unrest began downtown; the Arabs attacked the Jews indiscriminately. The Israeli Defense Forces (*Hagana, Palmach, Etzel*), who were better trained and organized, fought back, defending themselves. The Jewish defense forces became stronger day by day and well organized. This resulted in victories. Some of the Palestinian Arab leaders panicked, telling the Arab population to flee. Some left for Jordan, Lebanon, or Syria.*

The rest is history—an independent Jewish state!

On the third day after our arrival to Haifa, I was summoned to the yards of the Tecnion, one of the Hagana *command centers in Haifa, which was almost across the street from our hotel. A number of others gathered at the same time. We were given a briefing as to the reason we were called; that is, the Arab population downtown was organizing an uprising against the Jewish population. They said, "We need you all to be available to defend the Jewish population. We will meet every Sunday morning to give you your specific assignments." Another person and I were ordered that same day to go to a post established near the Arab market. We headed down town armed with two hand grenades and one old single shot British rifle. Our shift was from 12:00 noon until 10:00 PM when we were relieved by two others. This assignment was to be repeated day after day unless otherwise ordered. As I had weapon training, confidence, and a will to do my part for a safe homeland, I was glad to report to my position.*

Sara remained in the hotel resting and waiting for my homecoming. We were in the hotel ten days. Soon we received instructions from the immigration office that we were assigned to move to camp, Bat Galim, *which was converted from a British military camp to a new commerce center,* Beit Olim *(House of Immigrants), in the suburb of Haifa. By now Sara was happy to move anywhere, but not to a kibbutz. I had discussed my desire to go to the kibbutz where I had friends from the underground, Kibbutz Frumka. Sara was determined, as she explained to me with tears in her eyes, "I love you, but don't force me to a community life in a kibbutz after what I have experienced in my life. If you wish to go, I cannot hold you back. I will come to visit you," Sara said with good humor. I saw that she was upset. We stopped the conversation on this subject.*

Sara said, "I promise to do anything to help us to establish a warm friendly home. I am willing to work, so you need to find a job for me."

"What can you do with no profession?" I asked. Sara's reply was: "I worked near Buchenwald Concentration Camps in an ammunition factory.

Yes, I know how to make bullets and assemble grenades."

I said, "Great! I know there is a factory near Haifa. It is underground and managed by the Haganah (defense forces) I will get in touch with them in due time."

Well, the observation camp in Bat Galim was not a hotel. However, it was decent. We had a bed in a wooden military barrack, in a room with eight other couples. The meals were well balanced: bread, margarine, bananas, oranges, and tangerines, pasta, rice, potatoes, and vegetables. We were definitely not hungry. Our modest needs and expectations were satisfied.

With my contacts I became aware that new housing was being built for new immigrants. I signed up, and six months later we were taken to our new home. This was great; no money was needed. Everything was financed by the immigration authorities. What more could we want? We were also given a bed, a wooden table, and four chairs. The name of the town was Tiv'on (founded in 1947). Across the road was the <u>old</u> established town of Kiryat-Amal (founded in 1937)

ᴖ Chapter 19 ᴖ

There and Back Again

Israel, 1955: L to R Shifra Almogi, Stewart,
Yosef Almogi, Minister of Labor, Ernest, Sara

After his visit to the United States, when Ernest went back to Israel as a volunteer during the Sinai War in 1956, life in Israel was not the same. Before he left Israel, he had an important position. When Ernest left, people in politics wanted his job—they told stories such as: "He is never coming back." When he returned, Ernest did get another job; however, he was not satisfied with this job. Every time he returned from work, I saw that his heart was bleeding. I saw his pain. I said to him, "Ernest, you are not happy. Let's go back to the United

States. We will work hard and save money and then come back with enough money to be independent and to start a business." He replied, "Let's go to a *kibbutz*." I said, "No." So we returned to the U.S. One year there. One year here. Then back again.

When we came back to the U.S., my husband's brother, Villi, was helpful.

We came back with $35.00 between the two of us. I decided to borrow some money. I opened a stand on Marshall Street in Philadelphia. While our two children went to school, I became a businesswoman. It was hard but compared to before it was paradise.

At Christmas, it was very cold, and I was very thin; I felt the cold even more so. However, I did a terrific business selling. My husband bought close outs—toys and gift items. We decided to open a store.

We opened the store. Ernest then decided to make hula-hoops. In the evenings we made them and then loaded up the station wagon to sell them. We did so well I was able to pay $150.00 in

Philadelphia, 1960: Friends.
Sara and Ernest in the middle of the second row.

taxes to the government. I cried. I paid the $150.00. We did it! From ashes, I have done and I am able to do. I have drive!

Philadelphia, November 27, 1963: Sara's
citizenship document

Philadelphia: L to R, first row, Augi, Francis,
Munci, Sara, Lili; second row, Steven, Villi, Ernest, Emil

$\circledcirc$ Chapter 20 $\circledcirc$

Antisemitism

In America, Stewart and Dahlia started school. They needed help in English. I got them help. Dahlia was in a school in Philadelphia. Her teacher, however, was antisemitic. The teacher would not let her raise her hand. She said to Dahlia, "Sit down." Then the teacher called me into school. She said, "When does your daughter go to bed?" I said, "She goes to bed at 7:00 PM; we have strict rules. The teacher asked, "Then why is she falling asleep in school?" The teacher did not pay attention to her; therefore, she was bored and fell asleep.

I knew my rights. This is a free country—the United States. I asked for a meeting with the principal. We had our meeting. The principal told me, "Dahlia will be moved out of that class to a class with other Israeli kids." The teacher was fired. Dahlia bloomed. She became the best in English.[48]

When Dalia was twelve and Stewart was eight, my husband decided that we should have another child. I asked him, "Do we really want to start again?" My daughter said, "A dog or a baby." Stewart said, "Me too." My husband said, "Three dogs or one baby." I agreed to have another child because so many children had been lost during the Holocaust that we should have another child. This was a democratic decision.

I was thirty-three then. I got pregnant. My daughter and I wanted a girl, and my husband and Stewart wanted a boy. Gil was born with lots of love. Our daughter, Dahlia, said, "This is my baby!" She really cared for him as if he were hers.

Ernest changed professions. He went into the ceramics business, in which he prospered. We have built a life. We have three wonderful children and six grandchildren. In July 1995, we celebrated our fiftieth anniversary. Our granddaughter married a month later. She said, "What better gift! You have showed us a marriage of fifty years." Many friends and family were at our anniversary.

The Holocaust took everything from me but I have been given so much since then. With all the nightmares and pain of discovering my two brothers—all pain, I have tried to make peace. I try to tell people: Talk. Do not fight. Dialogue not violence! I have taught my children not to hate. I have taught them to give *tzedakah* (charity); it is important to help mankind.

For Dahlia: I love you so much—my miracle.

For Stewart: I love you so much—my pride.

For Gil: You are always my baby. I have a special love for you. I am very proud of you.

My three children have become terrific people, caring people. They have given me six grandchildren. I am so proud of them; they have all grown up to be wonderful people. How much I love and care for them!

Part Two

The following chapters were written by Ernest Paul.

Chapter 21

Sara's Kitchen

One of Sara's hobbies was cooking, not only cooking but cooking with love—a warm heart, good taste, and talent. I called the small kitchen in The Corinthian, our New York apartment, "the factory." Sara fed me; she spoiled me with her cooking and baking throughout over sixty years of marriage.

My favorite dish was her chicken soup with thin noodles. During the winter or summer, this chicken soup scented the apartment, a scent of love and taste even through summer nights in Atlantic City. Sara liked other soups also, such as vegetable, barley with bean, potato, cold borscht with warm potatoes. However, she never failed to offer me chicken soup with ratech (horseradish roots). Horseradish roots sliced thin and lightly salted were served with the chicken soup that was always available, if not from the stove then from the freezer. Sara enjoyed watching me eating, sitting beside me. When our kids, Dahlia, Stewart, and Gil lived at home, they were all spoiled, each one with her or his favorite dishes or delicious pastry.Sara's greatest naches (pride) was when she saw us eating and enjoying to our fullest. The hunger she suffered during the war lived in her all of her life. Feeding us as she did was her best remedy.

The growth of the kitchen's capacity came as our children married. They blessed us with six grandchildren and subsequently five great grandchildren. "Thank g-d, I have more hungry people to feed," Sara said. I needed to buy a second refrigerator and freezer and reorganize the kitchen to enable Sara to increase the kitchen capacity for cooking and baking.

As each child and grandchild grew up on mom-mom's yiken (chicken) soup and all the other goodies, they said, "Mom-mom's soup is the best in the world."

After swallowing each spoonful, all the kids raved. While each one developed a taste for his or her favorite food, chicken soup was a favorite. By no means did it end there; this was just the beginning.

After the soup came mom-mom's appetizers: salads, side dishes, such as hummus, chopped chicken liver, gefilte fish, red chrain (horseradish cooked with beets), stuffed mushrooms, cucumber salad, potato salad, *Gezer* Chai (literally, "live" carrot salad) Waldorf salad, fruit salad, potato kugel, latkes, and blintzes.

Then there were the special main courses, Sara's specialties: Chicken Paprikash, Stuffed Cabbage, *chulent* with meat and beans, stuffed barbecue chicken, Tahini pine nuts hamburger, special roast beef, and cabbage and noodles.

The holidays we celebrated as a family—together. This was always very important for Sara, spiritually, mentally and physically. If there was a cloud gathering over the holiday festivities, it was Sara looking into the future with tears in her eyes asking, "What will happen when I am gone? You all must promise me this tradition must go on. This reflects on our past when we lost our families. The holidays signify the presence of a beautiful family, growing up from the ashes of the crematoriums, the future of a growing traditional Jewish family—*lamrot hakol*—despite everything."

We all promised and lived up to our promises, in particular, my loving daughter Dahlia and my beloved daughters in law, Dali and Nancy. Each holiday rotates to their homes.

Passover specialties included baked rolls from *matzah* flour, a hundred or so rolls, and *matzah*—chocolate layer cake, ten cakes. After all, the rolls and *matzah* cake had to last throughout the holiday for all of us. Then there were homemade egg noodles for the chicken soup. To prepare all this at home would mean that Sara usually started ten days before. I was licking my fingers every day from the chocolate cream.

Rosh HaShanah (the Jewish New Year) specialties were chopped liver, chicken soup of course, gefilte chicken, zucchini casserole, vegetable casserole, potato *kugel, latkes,* and sweet potatoes.

Sara cooked not only for Jewish holidays but also for national holidays such as Thanksgiving. First was Sara's famous soup with thin noodles; then the two 15-20 lb turkeys that were baked to mouthwatering perfection; and her unique stuffing loved by all. The carving of the turkey was, and still is, my job. In addition was the colorful carved out watermelon filled with the nicest fruits of the season. That was also a conservation piece in the center of the table. On *Chanukah* were *latkes* and more *latkes* with sour cream or apple sauce.

To top the above, during the holidays, were Sara's mouth watering home baked pastries. The hot apple strudel, *makosh* rolled chocolate sponge cake filled with fine ground poppy seeds, nuts, or chocolate, and *kremesh*, a typical Hungarian specialty.

Sara cooked and baked all year around. She was well equipped with hermetically closed containers which rotated all year among our kids and Sara. Fortunately our kids worked with me in our business in New York, so they were the delivery service in this well planned system of Sara's. For the holiday we hired a car service to take us and the prepared food to the specific home that we rotated to each holiday.

One of Sara's most difficult tasks the last years was to remember what each child requested because some were vegetarians. We always appreciated her efforts.

We will miss you, my beloved Sara!

Chapter 22

Sara's Recipes

The following are excerpted from the recipe book Sara gave each of the children. They are her most loved recipes.

Tender Loving Care Recipes

To All My Children,

Here are my recipes. Hopefully, you will all find something you like and will use. I have included recipes from home, from Czechoslovakia and from Israel. I am going to give you everything I can remember. I hope that you will find something to your liking. If not, maybe my grandchildren, great-grandchildren, and future generations will enjoy some of these dishes.

I love you all very much, Remember, every time you use one of my recipes, there was a "loving mother, grandmother, and great-grandmother" and she did a half decent job cooking.

Sara Paul

Dedication

I thought what better way is there to honor my "Ima" on her seventy- something birthday than to finally record her recipes. These recipes nourished us all through winter colds, quirky diets, and allowed for beautiful holiday celebrations and lovely Sunday brunches, picnics, and barbecues.

It was a project begun sometime ago by someone else, but never finished. Nor did that early version capture the essential ingredient in every recipe – a mother's love. Standing in her little New York kitchen, not only were recipes from "home" recreated but also many new ones were developed to satisfy our ever changing requests: more protein, less fat, fat is okay (Stewart only), only whole grain carbs. The vegetarians in our midst put in their requests for dishes with tofu, but not eggs, with eggs, but not tofu, with tofu, but not spinach… and no beans, thank-you. Some of the recipes reflect the changing pattern of eating in America itself as in the recommended use of artificial sweeteners and margarine, lite versions of things.

Each dish was prepared with enthusiasm, generosity, and amazing talent. Each dish was prepared in such abundance as to provide leftovers for days to come, for the freezer, for the neighbors, for friends. Which of our friends has not greeted their first taste of Matzah cake with exclamations of "I didn't know matzah was capable of this?" Only in the hands of Sara Paul would matzah be capable of such a wondrous taste.

So here are the recipes in all their delectable glory. Having personally sampled just about every dish many times over, I say "Hail to the Chef," and "B'Tayavon."

Nancy Z. Paul

Chicken Soup

2 whole chickens
1 ½ lb top rib of beef
2-3 turkey wings
2 Beef Bones
2-3 cloves of garlic
Pepper to taste
1 pkg carrots
3 onions
7 stalks celery
3 turnips
3 zucchini
½ green pepper
4-5 parsnips
Parsley and dill (2 bunches each)
8-10 Telma chicken soup cubes
½ jar chicken soup

Wash and dice vegetables, add to pot with chicken, turkey, bones, and meat and cover with water. Add soup cubes and ½ jar of soup. Simmer on stove until meat is tender. When it's almost done, add parsley and dill, garlic and pepper.

Note: Soup can be frozen with meat. You can make barbecue chicken with the chicken (see below) or chicken salad.

Vegetarian Faux Chicken Soup

Use the same recipe for chicken soup less the meat and chicken soup. Add more vegetables for rich stock. Add 10 cubes of veggie bouillon power.

Mamaliga
4 cups skim milk
Salt to taste
2 cups cornmeal
Sour Cream
Cheese (variety of 3 cheeses such a Mozzarella, Swiss and Cheddar)

Mix milk, cornmeal and salt together, stirring frequently. Grease
casserole dish. Put a thin layer of cornmeal mixture on bottom of
casserole dish. Add 1 Tbsp soup cream. Top with 1 Tbsp each of
Mozzarella, Swiss, and Cheddar cheeses. Top casserole with sour
cream and cheeses. Bake at 350 degrees for 15-20 minutes. Casserole
should bake covered for first 5 minutes.

Hamburgers with Tahini and Pine Nuts
4 lbs ground beef
3 onions
4 cloves garlic
1 stalk celery
2 carrots
Paprika
Oil
Pepper
½ Tbsp Telman Onion Soup
4 eggs
2 ½ Tbsp Matzah meal
3 Tbsp Ketchup
4 Tbsp Tahini
3 Tbsp Water
Pine nuts

Very finely chop vegetables and sauté in oil and seasonings. Cool. Mix meat together with the vegetables, eggs, matzah meal, and ketchup. Form patties and fry covered in hot oil, turning once. Put hamburgers on paper towels to absorb oil. Mix together the Tahini and water and spoon over hamburgers. Top with pine nuts and bake for 6 minutes at 350°.

Vegetarian "Meatballs"
See above recipe. Replace meat with 1 container of tofu, sliced very thin.
Double the above vegetables and add others, like mushrooms and spinach.
4 eggs
3 Tbsp Matzah Meal
3 Tbsp tomato sauce
Pepper
Paprika
½ Tbsp Telma Onion Soup
Jar of tomato sauce with vegetables
Oil

Let tomato sauce simmer in pot. In separate frying pan sauté very finely chopped vegetable and tofu mixture in oil; add seasonings. Allow to cool. Add eggs, 3 Tbsp tomato sauce and matzah meal to mixture and let stand. Shape into round balls. Drop into pot of tomato sauce and simmer for 30 minutes. Add any leftover vegetables to flavor tomato sauce.

Veggie Burgers
Same as above, only shape into patties and fry in oil.

Matzah Cake

1½ cups Malaga wine, heated

Matzah (6 pieces per cake)

3 sticks butter

2 cups fudge

Dip Matzah into hot wine for just a moment. Matzah shouldn't be allowed to soften or break. Make a fluffy cream with the remaining ingredients. Cover each piece of matzah with cream and layer, covering the entire matzah tower with cream. Top with nuts, coconut, or chocolate – whatever you like.

Poppy Seed, Nut and Chocolate Roll Cakes

The following recipe will make 6 roll cakes, 2 of each kind.

Dough:

3 lbs flour

2 small pkgs dry yeast dropped into

½ cup warmed skim milk

¾ lb butter

1 Tbsp vanilla

½ tsp baking powder

¾ cup sugar

4 eggs (1 whole and 3 yokes)

Mix by hand until the dough is fine. Divide into 6 tennis size balls and refrigerate overnight. Roll dough out and fill.

Fillings:

Poppy seed – use 1 jar of poppy seeds per roll

Nut – 1 10 oz bag of finely crushed walnuts mixed with ½ cup sugar and lemon zest.

Chocolate – 1 cup of bittersweet chocolate mixed with ½ cup sugar. Dot the dough that will contain the chocolate filling first with margarine, then spread the chocolate mixture, and top with 2 oz of grape jelly.

All the dough, once filled, should be rolled slowly by hand squeezing the ends closed so as to keep the filling in. Make tiny holes with a fork in the dough so steam can escape. Bake at 350 degrees for one hour. Take out and brush with mixture made of 1 egg yoke, a drop of sugar and a drop of water. Return to oven for another 15 minutes until golden brown.

ᏹᐧᐧChapter 23 ᐧᐧᏹ

Sara's Exercise Program

At age forty, before any of us, family or friends, were even thinking of physical fitness, Sara made a commitment to physical activity; it became her "religion."

During the winter her days started at 6:00 AM with one hour/ 5 miles on the treadmill; a 45 minutes aerobics classes; and one additional hour walking on the indoor tracks. Because we lived in the Corinthian Condos in New York, we had access to a great gym. During the summer months she walked the Atlantic City boardwalk, "This I am doing for Sara Paul," she used to say.

Not only did she religiously live up to her commitment, but she got me on "track." She tried to put me on her schedule. I have to admit that I could not keep up with her; I did only the weekends, treadmill one hour, water aerobics, and walking—sometimes, "schlepping" on the boardwalk.

Sara influenced her friends and neighbors, and as our kids grew older she was a role model for them. Dahlia loved to work out with her mom. Her belief in the value of physical activity trickled down even to our oldest grandchildren, Tara and Ilana. Sara was an inspiration in this as in all things.

In the Corinthian Condo gym, year after year, Sara won awards for being the most active and consistent participant.

During the summer months we lived in Atlantic City at the Ocean Club condos, where we also had excellent instructors and a gym at our disposal. Sara was the

Ocean Club, Atlantic City, 1996:
L to R Betty, Ilane, Sara, Louise, Paula

envy of all the women and a shining example for her discipline and accomplishments.

Five of her friends were her steady exercise partners; however, none of them could keep up with Sara, particularly when she added to the summer activity a daily one hour water aerobics with the supervision of a professional teacher.

When Sara walked on the boardwalk, many heads turned—not only men but also women. Some turned in support; some, in jealousy. They remarked, "How can she do it every day, seven days a week?" If it was 6 AM, Sara was out there with me, or without me (during weekdays). She had a recognizable posture, her walk exuded elegance, glamour, and confidence. Neither the boardwalk nor the aerobic classes on the 6th floor will ever be the same, since she is gone.

Sara was passionate for music, our son Gil bought her an iPod and recorded hundreds of Sara's favorite songs. I walked with Sara on the weekends mostly; we listened to some of the same music but not necessarily at the same beat. I could not keep up with her vigorous marching.

When Sara traveled with me on my many business trips, she always insisted on a spacious room in the hotel, so we could do daily aerobics in the room. At that time there were no gyms in the hotels. She never failed to carry with her the "gear": workout suits and her favorite music for aerobics.

From time to time we were entertained late into the night. In South America dinners never start before 9:00. PM, so the entertainment ran into the early hours of the morning. As did the food!

The thirty plus options on the salad bar were followed with endless chicken and sausages, all wonderfully grilled and served on skewers hot to the table. While good wines helped to digest the food, consumption of the traditional *caipirinha*, the national cocktail of Brazil, a sugar cane alcohol drink, did not help to get me up with Sara at 6:00 AM.[49] Because Sara drank neither wine nor other alcohol, she had no problem. Only I had the hangovers.

༶ Chapter 24 ༶

Our 62 Year Marriage

Throughout the years we had our ups and downs, as do most normal marriages. The beginning was relatively smooth and "rosy" in spite of the illness of Sara. For two years I nurtured her throughout her illness with TB. We managed to discuss issues as they arose and resolve them amicably.

Sara was the "Boss" at home. I accepted her role as such from day one. Sara was in charge of every aspect of the household. She handled the family budget responsibly, she paid the bills, and she did all of the shopping for food, clothing, and other necessities.

Sara was in charge of moving our home numerous times: in Philadelphia we moved three times, then a move to New York, and within New York we moved twice. Sara was in charge of furnishing and decorating our homes, including our summer homes in Atlantic City, from the Roosevelt Condos to Margate Towers and finally the Ocean Club Condos. Sara's taste and style were reflected in every move.

Sara was also the handyman; at home, she changed light bulbs, replaced missing screws, fixed the sliding windows, and on and on. She never ceased to amaze me and surprise me.

I was never home for any move or to share the daily issues of home life. She almost single handedly raised our three wonderful children, suffering with them in their childhood illnesses and pain. I did share the results, the satisfaction and enjoyment we got from the kids: Birthdays, Graduations, *Bar/Bat Mitzvah,* and Weddings.

My major concern was striving to provide a decent living standard for my family and the best education for our kids even under the most difficult circumstances. Most of my years in business (sixty years out of sixty-two years of marriage) involved traveling overseas or in the U.S. This traveling definitely took a toll on the children as well as Sara and me.

Thanks to Sara's strength and my determination we managed through "thick and thin," in sunny days as well as stormy days. For the first years of traveling overseas I always managed to put a positive spin on my absence, taking advantage of some of the good duty free shops and buying Sara her favorite perfumes and jewelry. I brought her something from each country and also for my kids, in particular for my daughter, Dahlia, and my granddaughters—dolls from each country.

The reunions, my homecomings, were always happy occasions, "a honeymoon," a reason to celebrate. I gained more confidence and made friends in the countries I traveled to including Brazil, Chile, Argentina, Peru, Colombia, Germany, Italy, England, The Netherlands, and Israel. I invited Sara to travel with me.

From time to time the planning of these trips was difficult, but the trips were always enjoyable because they gave us the opportunity to spend quality time together.

The intricate part of business involved traveling to work with our people in the Primex offices in Israel, Brazil, Argentina, Chile, Peru, Colombia, and Mexico, as well as traveling with buyers and visiting, both internationally and in the U.S. Whenever possible I combined business with pleasure by having Sara along on my trips.

The highlights of our trips were always the visits to Israel, where I traveled several times a year. Sara joined me every December for twenty-eight years to the Moria Resorts at the Dead Sea. We always went to the same hotel where I in particular enjoyed the salty sea, the mudpacks, massages, the two hour daily ping pong tournament that I won several times. Above all the bright sunny days in Israel with Sara were very special to me. Sara did not like to participate in these activities. She said, "This sea vacation I am doing for you." Sara did enjoy the indoor sulfa pool and our time together.

It was like homecoming to go to the Moria Resort. We loved the good food and the service, and every evening we enjoyed the music—the singing and dancing in which we actively participated. We loved the Moria Hotel and the management, so we decided that one day we would have our first grandson, Ari's, *Bar Mitzvah* at the Moria and the religious services on the nearby historical mountains of *Masada* (Hebrew: *Metzada).*[50]

While in Israel, we also enjoyed Tel Aviv, visiting family and friends in Tel Aviv and Haifa. I also spent some time at our Primex office there.

Sara's travels with me reduced the tension between us. She loved shopping in each country for something specific. Israel was her favorite for Gotex bathing suits, jewelry, and Beged-Or leather apparel. Brazil was known for the wide range of precious and semi-precious stones, such as aquamarine, amethyst, and topaz; Argentina for leather goods, pocket books, leather boots, belts; London for rain coats; and Italy for clothing, shoes, and pocketbooks.

In each country we enjoyed the special foods at the numerous restaurants. Many of the trips were planned around the trade shows that I had to attend. This made it possible for us to spend more valuable time together. In each country, within my time constraints, we planned visits to museums, theatres, and concerts. This part was always the carrot that sweetened our traveling, for Sara loved the arts. Often we planned our trips to visit famous spas such as at Israel's Dead Sea and the Czech Republic's Karlovy Vary (known in English as Carlsbad), where the natural hot spring water flows from the ground. The baths healed the outside and the water fountains throughout the city healed the inside. We also went to the spas in Budapest and Brazil.

Sara went with me to trade shows. Twice a year we went to the International Frankfurt and the Chicago Housewares Show. The latter always took place around January 14, my birthday, and around July 13, our wedding anniversary. We all went: Sara, Stewart, Gil, Steve, my brother Emil, and other members of our team. The trade shows in Chicago were the most important events in our business; each show had over 2,000 exhibitors and over 50,000 buyers from all over the U.S., Canada, and other countries. Our company, the Primex/American Heritage Company, had a strong clientele following.

The show was held at the McCormick Exhibition Center on the Michigan Lake, always starting on a Sunday and ending on Wednesday. We had to arrive on Friday to help set up. In January it was ten to twenty below zero; in July, in the mid eighties.

In order to meet our customers in a private environment after the show closed in the evening, we occupied a large suite and had twelve rooms to network and show our appreciation to our customers. The buffet setting at the hotel across from the exhibit hall was rich, tasteful, with plenty of food and drinks, wines, liquors, champagne, etc. This was Sara's job to supervise.

At 7:30 in the evening we had a special dinner with specific customers and suppliers. Chicago was known for a great variety of restaurants such as the "Bakery" for Hungarian Cuisine; however, our favorite was the Italian Village on Monroe Avenue. I had visited the

Italian Village for over fifty years, so I know the owners well, three generations of Frankie's. The restaurant was in a beautiful Italian three-story building with three different restaurants with three different managers. Our choice was always the second floor.

When we called for reservations for Mr. Paul, there was always room. Most of the time we had a private room that seated thirty people; we filled every chair. The food and the special service we received from the owners and the maitre d' were second to none. When the Paul family with our guests walked in, all their attention was given to us. The maitre d' had lined up numerous bottles of our favorite chilled white wines and rich aroma red Italian wines.

The inside of the restaurant was furbished with rich Italian wood, gold leaf covered wood carvings, almost like a richly decorated church. The wall décor was warm and pleasing. The overall atmosphere with the lighting and the music was an experience in itself. Then came the food.

The freshly prepared anti-pastas with extra large shrimp and Italian cold cuts were always a great start followed by a mouth-watering wine. The main course was offered with a singsong, heavy Italian accent by the head maitre d" Lorenzo. When it came to the steady visitors, Lorenzo told us what to eat. We always had the best.

At Frankie's the accordion player was Bartello. When we arrived, he dropped everything, playing and serenading us all evening. He knew that January was my birthday; July, our anniversary. This restaurant was also Sara's favorite. We had many, many memorable evenings in this place. Our dancing and singing came spontaneously after we emptied a few bottles of wine.

In 1978 Bartello retired, however, he knew the dates of the Housewares Show and knew Mr. Paul would be coming to the restaurant. He left a strict message to the owner Frankie to call him when we arrived. Then Bartello showed up with his accordion and entertained us for hours.

These were just some of the fringe benefits of meeting and knowing a large number of people. Many of them became our good friends until this day.

During the last year of Sara's illness I stopped traveling and dedicated myself to her care. My love for her grew stronger and stronger every year reaching its peak before her last breath.

⊗·· Chapter 25 ··⊗

Our 50ᵗʰ Anniversary

Fifty years ago I had promised Sara that one day we would have a "real" wedding with a rabbi to make up for the wedding we did not have when on July 13, 1945, our friend Zvi Prizant in *Kibbutz Frumka,* Bucharest, declared and recognized by his authority as head of the *kibbutz* (captain of the ship) for us to live together as a couple.

Almost to the date I kept my promise—on July 15, 1995. We had our Rabbi Goldman from the Adat-Zion Congregation in Philadelphia, where we use to belong, come especially to officiate and legitimize our marriage.

The religious ceremony was very moving for Sara and me as well as our kids, in particular to "legitimize" Mom and Dad's marriage. The presence of my sister, Chaja, her husband, Avraham, who came especially from Israel, as well as our dear friends Yocheved and Zvi Prizant (the rabbi of our first wedding in Bucharest) meant a great deal to us.

My brother Villi, his wife, Munci, and their children, Miriam and Steven; my brother, Emil, his wife, Lili, with their three kids, Rifka, David, and Neal, were a blessing. Sara's cousin, Sara Rasmovich Brownstein from Florida, their son, Michel, and his wife, Ilene; my friend from the bunker, Andi, his wife, Eata; our dear friends Ursula and her father, Klaus Schumacher, from Brazil; from Chile our friend

Juan Eduardo, Christian, Isabel Lanas, Petrito Fernandez; from St. Louis, Don Ranz, his wife, Carrie, Marie Murphy; our three children and their families: Dahlia, her daughters, Tara and Ilana; Stewart and Nancy with their sons, Ari and Eitan; Gil, Dali, their daughter, Elite; our cousins, the Grosses, the many, many friends from New York and Philadelphia; our neighbors from the Ocean Club, in particular Barry, Rachel, their son, Ely, daughters, Tova and Jeannet; our friends Zig and Paula Menash; John Dennes, his wife, Ilene—and all the many others (over 250) filled our hearth with love, appreciation, and friendship. The beautifully decorated banquet hall at the Atlantic City Tropicana Hotel and Casino, the great Kantor band from Philadelphia, the cocktails, the excellent food, and, above all, our beautifully dressed family members and friends certainly made it worthwhile to wait fifty years. It was a most memorable event; we are appreciative and grateful to all.

Our Jewish tradition teaches us that in times of celebration, we should always remember those who are not able to be with us.

Or fiftieth wedding anniversary coincided with another historic date, the end of World War II and the fiftieth anniversary of the liberation of the Nazi camps.

We asked our guests the following:

> As survivors of the Holocaust, during which most of our families perished, we feel a sense of mission to combine these two dates in a meaningful way. We would appreciate and be very thankful if any gift honoring our fiftieth anniversary would go as a contribution to a unique educational program that prepares high school teachers to implement Holocaust studies in their classes on the Holocaust and Jewish Resistance.
>
> This project is very important and close to our hearts. Please direct any gifts as a contribution to this

special, tax deductible program. Checks should be made out to the American Gathering of Jewish Holocaust Survivors Education.

So fifty years later, on July 15, 1995, we were officially married in the Tropicana Hotel Casino in Atlantic City by Rabbi Goldberg from Adat Zion Congregation in Philadelphia. In the presence of 250 friends; our three children, Dahlia, Stewart and Gil; their wives; and five grandchildren, Tara, Ilana, Ari, Eitan, Elite, and Daniel, we celebrated our marriage.

I had kept my promise!

Fiftieth Wedding Anniversary, July 15, 1995:
L to R Sara, Bernie, Edith, and Ernest

✣ Chapter 26 ✣

Trip to Remember

For our fiftieth wedding anniversary, our son Stewart initiated and planned a trip for us half way around the world— a first class round trip, with the excellent Australian airline, Qantas.

The three weeks trip started in New York, went to San Francisco, then to Honolulu, Hawaii, and Melbourne, Australia, from there to Sidney, Australia, and on to Beijing, China, then to Hong Kong, to Taiwan, Japan, and back home. In each city we spent valuable time with professional tour guides. As I learned long ago, to get the most out of these trips hire a local guide or join an official tour in each city. There is no better way.

We immensely enjoyed visiting each country, the museums, and the rich historical landmarks. The highlight of the trip for Sara was San Francisco (Sara's first time), Honolulu, Sidney, Australia, and, in China, the historical Forbidden City, the Great Wall and mosques, churches, and temples.

The hotel accommodations were all five stars. We enjoyed the beautiful beaches, restaurants, and cultural activities.

This was a once in a lifetime, an unforgettable trip!

❧ · Chapter 27 · ❧

Sara's Last Struggle

One of Sara's favorite poems was about growing old.

I'm Fine.
There is nothing whatever the matter with me;
I am just as healthy as I can be.
I have arthritis in both of my knees,
And when I talk, I talk with a wheeze.
My pulse is weak, and my blood is thin,
But I'm awfully well for the shape I'm in.

My teeth eventually have to come out
And my Diet – I hate to think about!
I am overweight and I can't get thin,
But I'm awfully well for the shape I'm in.

I think my liver is out of whack,
And a terrible pain is in my back.
My hearing is poor, my sight is dim,
Most everything seems to be out of trim,
But I'm awfully well for the shape I'm in.

I have arch supports for both of my feet,
Or I wouldn't be able to go on the street,
Sleeplessness I have, night after night,
And in the morning I'm just a sight,
My memory's failing, my head's in a spin,
But I'm awfully well for the shape I'm in.

The moral is, as this tale we unfold,
That for you and me, who are growing old,
It's better to say "I'm fine" with a grin
Then to let them know the shape we're in.

At the end of 2007, Sara was not in good shape and was not able to tell me that she was "fine." Sara complained of losing weight, feeling tired, and having headaches. So, on December 15, 2007, I took Sara to our family doctor in New York, Dr. Mark Newman, who had been our doctor for over twenty years. He knew Sara well: her sense of humor, her smile, and the twinkle in her eyes. But he did not see these—not this time. This was not the same Sara.

After an examination and blood tests, Dr. Newman said, "I do not like what I see. You need to see a specialist." The doctor referred us to New York University (NYU) Oncology Department to Dr. Eliot Newman (the same last name but no relation to Dr. Mark Newman). The earliest appointment available was three days later on December 18.

As we took the elevator to the eighth floor both of our hearts were pounding. There was no waiting time. The doctor was there. After his own examination, the doctor took us into his office and told us to be seated, and we waited a few minutes for the test results from his lab. The fifteen minutes seemed to us like hours. In the meantime I tried to lift Sara's spirits. She was very depressed and concerned. So was I; however, I could not show my real emotions. I couldn't break down; I felt I had to be strong for Sara.

Dr. Newman returned to his office, sat down behind his desk in his comfortable chair, and then dropped a bombshell. He said, "I have bad news, Mrs. Paul. You have pancreatic cancer, and surgery is urgently required." Sara took a few deep breaths, and with her sense of humor, she told the doctor, "Cancer or no cancer we are scheduled to leave on a fourteen day cruise on the Queen Mary, December 22, four days from now. I definitely want to go on this cruise and spend these fourteen days with my husband."

Dr. Newman was surprised, flabbergasted, by Sara's reaction. Really, so was I. He said, "Well, it is your decision against my advice."

The doctor's determination started to sink in with us. I started questioning the doctor, "How long is this kind of surgery? What are her chances with or without surgery?"

Dr. Newman's answers were not encouraging. He said, "Without any surgery, you will live no longer than six months. The cancer could spread slower or faster. Pancreatic cancer is rarely curable—one in many thousands."

With tears in my eyes, I said to the doctor, "Sara is a concentration camp survivor. She has suffered a lot: typhus and tuberculosis. I cannot lose her now. We have three children, six grandchildren, and five great-grandchildren. She cannot die now."

The doctor stated with confidence, "I will try my very best. I promise both of you." Sara threw in a few Yiddish words to the relatively young doctor, about forty-eight years old. He replied in Yiddish: *"I'ch wel dire halfen"* (I will help you).

Sara took a liking to Dr. Newman. She asked him, "You could be my son. How would you treat your mother?" His reply was, "I will treat you with love and kindness." She replied, "Okay. We will be back from our cruise on January 9."

Last Cruise, December 22, 1997: Sara and Ernest

Dr. Newman looked at his computer calendar and gave us a date for the surgery, January 11, at 8:00 AM at NYU. We arrived on time, as did the doctor. The nurses started with the preparations for the surgery. Five hours later she came out of surgery. It took the doctors over two hours to wake Sara from the heavy dose of anesthesia. When she finally opened her eyes, around her were the children, Dahlia, Stewart, Nancy, Gil, Dali, and me. All had arrived while she was still in surgery. We were all stressed, hoping and crying. We were fearful. Did she survive? Was the surgeon able to excise the cancer? The doctor gave us no indication or sense of success. We needed to wait. Finally the surgeon advised us to go home, saying, "Sara will have to stay in the hospital for a while. In the next couple of days I will be able to share with you more as to her condition."

Sara was admitted to the intensive care unit on the twelfth floor in NYU. I stayed with her overnight in hope of some sign or indication from Sara as to her pain or feelings. She was heavily medicated, sleeping throughout most of the night. At 6:00 AM, Dr. Eliot Newman arrived with Dr. Alec Goldenberg and his associate, Dr. K. Haglof. "Dr. Goldenberg is a cancer specialist," I was told by Dr. Newman, "the best in his field."

Stewart arrived from his home in Princeton, New Jersey, around 6:30 AM, followed by Gil. We tried to get more information from the doctors; however, the only information we got, "We will do everything possible for her. She will need to stay in the hospital for a couple of weeks."

After three days Sara was moved from the intensive care unit to the sixteenth floor, the cancer patient's floor. Sara was receiving good care from the doctors and nurses. Her cardiologist, Dr K. Kraus, her lung specialist, Dr Camelhair, and her liver specialist, Dr. Tobias, were notified of Sara's hospitalization. They also made daily visits and kept an eye on Sara because she had been their patient for over twenty years. What made a bad situation more difficult were her heart murmur and a dangerously high cholesterol level; moreover, the removal of her pancreas made her a high-risk diabetic.

I was at Sara's bedside from 5:45 AM (waiting for the scheduled visit of the doctors at 6:00 AM), and I stayed until 8:00 PM. I was relieved by a private night nurse I had hired.

Sara's wound from the surgery was healing; however, she had no appetite. Sleepless nights, her worries, and concerns, kept her in pain. "What about the children and grandchildren? Do they know I am here?"

At first she did not realize that the children were at the hospital every day. Her concern for them overshadowed her pain. Four days later with the help of the nurse we started to walk her down the long hallways of the hospital.

I decided that the next thing she needed was to eat, so from the cafeteria I bought in fresh food, chicken soup, blintzes, grilled chicken, etc. Each day she nibbled away a little more. The hospital food was not to her liking at all, despite the fact that a dietician from the hospital staff came to her bedside asking her, "What would you like to eat? We will be glad to make anything you like."

Sara was hooked up to monitors, receiving intravenous fluids and medications. She stayed in the hospital a total of fourteen days.

After the fifth or sixth day, before I left the hospital that evening, I was given an order by Sara, "In the morning, please bring me my folding mirror, my blue bathrobe, my slippers, my makeup kit, two hair brushes, tooth brush, and tooth paste." I was glad to get this order because this was a signal of hope and will power. This was my Sara. Even while facing this serious illness, she never lost her self-confidence and her desire to maintain her elegant appearance.

Before leaving the hospital, the surgeon, Dr Newman, told us, "I did my utmost to clean out the cancer. In these cases there is no 100%.

Let's hope for the best. From now on, you will now be in the hands of Dr Goldberg for treatments."

We showed up in Dr Goldberg's clinic where the nurses already had Sara's files with instructions about the treatment prescribed. They sat her in a comfortable chair among ten other cancer patients. The nurse rolled up Sara's sleeve, looked for a good vein, which was difficult to find, so they decided to insert a port for easy daily access to her collapsed veins. The treatment was painless; it took two hours until the large bottle was emptied drop by drop.

After this first treatment, Stewart, Sara, and I took the elevator to the fourth floor to meet with Dr Goldberg. We asked questions about how long and how often Sara would have to take these treatments? "We will see how she reacts," answered the doctor. "For now she will start with every day. Often we need to adjust the medication depending on the patient's reaction. As to a timetable, at this stage we cannot predict this. We will take one day at a time."

We took Sara home. She felt dizzy, so we put her in bed. In the evening she had a 102° temperature, as the doctor had cautioned us. The high temperature was expected. I called the doctor in the evening. He told me to give her two Tylenols and come in the morning. During the visit her fever subsided, and treatment was repeated. In the evening she was hot again with a 101° temperature. We repeated the Tylenol.

She had a restless night. She had no appetite to eat.

The doctor told us the following morning, "This is to be expected." He prescribed a sleeping pill and relaxing medication. The fever continued.

After the first week, the doctor told us he would change the mix of her medication and would continue to adjust as needed. He cautioned Sara, "You also must realize that in a few weeks, you will lose your hair gradually."

Sara was not a happy camper. For six weeks the treatments were daily. Sara did not get better.

The doctor told us that additional lab tests were required: M.R.I., CAT Scans, etc, He said that he was readmitting her to the hospital for a few days. While in the hospital, chemo treatments continued for six days with no noticeable improvement. Then treatments resumed in the doctor's clinic. By now Sara had made good friends with all the staff, with the receptionist, and nurses.

She became a "favorite" patient, referred to as the model of elegance, a showgirl. Sara amused the staff and the other patients with her elegance, her chic appearance. Each day the dress had to match the high leather boots or shoes and a matching pocketbook. A different glittering pin on her lapel was a surprise. As if in a fashion show she walked beautifully, with poise and elegance. She was well known and loved in the clinic. Sara tried to hide her problems with her appearance. She not only carried her slim body gracefully, but she also became a vital spirit with her unusual sense of humor. When she was getting treatments between two other patients, she always carried on uplifting, encouraging conversations with the other patients. Every one rushed to be near her. The nurses told me, "Sara is a healing element; the place lights up when Sara walks in." Sara tried to make the best of a difficult and depressing atmosphere.

She continued suffering from a lack of appetite, continued loss of weight and loss of hair. The loss of hair occurred faster than expected. Dahlia, our daughter, took her mom one day to a custom wig place; she convinced Sara to have one made for her (human hair). Sara wore the expensive wig once. She did not like the wig (like a *sheytl*); neither did I. The following day she donated the wig to some patient that wanted one but could not afford it. I helped her brush the few hairs she had left. This did not bother us. The bigger picture was our concern.

After all, what is hair loss compared to life.

Sara continued the chemo treatment for ten months. However, on November 18, 2007, she became very ill. Nonetheless, Sara was determined to leave the hospital in order to celebrate Thanksgiving with her beloved family. Somehow we traveled to Cherry Hill, New Jersey, and enjoyed the day with our children, grandchildren, and great-grandchildren. She sat erect, her head held high, red lipstick on, nails polished, and never uttered a word about how she was feeling. She enjoyed watching her three "daughters"—Dahlia, Nancy, and Dali—share the responsibility of carrying on the holiday traditions. Nancy likes to say that it takes three sisters to do half the job one mom did. It was the last time our beloved Sara would share a holiday with us.

The treatments had not answered our prayers. She was readmitted to NYU Hospital. The doctors shared with us that the treatments had failed to improve her condition. Various new tests were done as they tried to establish a different treatment.

Sara was very sick. As I watched her for days, weeks, and months fading away, staying in the hospital at her bedside, watching her pain and suffering, I broke down. I was hospitalized in a room next to Sara's for three weeks. At first it was weakness—exhaustion, the doctors told me. That was followed by a series of small seizures in my brain; the impact was waves of electrical shocks. When the children came to visit Sara, we were in ajoining rooms. Sara and I visited each other in wheel chairs.

Sara's illness took a heavy toll on me. My watching her suffering for almost a year weakened my strong immune system and my personality. I lost over 25 lbs watching her helpless suffering. Sitting side by side in our wheel chairs, Sara poured her heart out, "Oh G-d, how much I would like to live to see my granddaughter Elite on her sixteenth birthday and, above all, to be at my youngest grandchild's, Daniel's, *Bar*

Mitzvah (Elite and Daniel are Dali and Gil's daughter and son). Sara cried and spoke with a weak fading voice.

I pulled myself together, wiped her tears, and tried to find encouraging words, as I always did. But not this time! I suddenly choked. I became speechless, knowing we had reached the end.

Soon after this, Sara completely stopped eating. The doctors stopped the chemo treatments. She continued to fade away day by day.

On January 17, at 3:30 AM, Sara was pronounced dead.

At the Goldstein Funeral Home in Philadelphia on January 21, 2008, there was a moving outpouring of friends and family, almost 300 people.

The eulogies delivered by our children and grandchildren were delivered with tears and with love from the depths of their hearts. They reflected on their mom, Mom-Mom Sara: about how much they loved her, how much they respected her, how much she meant to them, and how much they will miss her forever.

The service at the cemetery followed with sitting *Shiva* at the house of our daughter, Dahlia, in Cherry Hill, New Jersey. Many friends came during the week.

There were hundreds of sympathy cards, especially touching letters, testimonials from friends in the U.S., and from numerous countries that Sara visited during her life, Israel, Brazil, Chile, Peru, Colombia, and Mexico.

As we lived the first thirty years of our time in the U.S., in Philadelphia, we had belonged to the Adat-Zion Congregation on Friendship Street in Philadelphia. We had purchased our gravesites in this community where Sara now rests for eternity. May she rest in peace.

I lost a partner of sixty-two years. My kids, grandkids, and great-grandkids lost a loving Mom-Mom Savta, the best in the world.

Our loss will stay with us forever and ever.

·· Chapter 28 ··

Eulogies and Condolences

Stewart's Words:

How can a successful life be measured? It can only be measured by what we leave behind: Friends and family, the lives we influence, and leaving the world a better place for having taken action and loved. What can I say about Mom? She meant so much to all of us. She touched our lives every day and in so many ways. She left her mark in the world. Mom was one of the most successful people I have ever known. She was a fighter. She never gave up. She overcame the loss of her home, she overcame concentration camps, she overcame the loss of her family, she overcame poverty, she overcame illness and even with her last battle with cancer she beat the odds. She held out longer then expected. During all of her trials and tribulations, those around her rarely knew of her problems. She always was there to support others and requested so little for herself.

In a few short months, we witnessed how her health deteriorated. But her spirit was always there. She always said, "Where there is life there is hope." She held out for Thanksgiving Dinner with the whole family. She knew this would be her true farewell, even though she would linger on another few weeks.

Mom didn't just fight, she didn't settle for survival. Mom and Dad's devotion to one another was not only touching but also inspirational. Mom and Dad built a family that anyone would be proud of: children, grandchildren, even great-grandchildren who adored her, and friends and family that both loved and respected her. Passing acquaintances, neighbors, and more recently doctors and nurses cared for her, truly cared for her. Mom could meet a stranger and in a few short moments become a lifelong friend. When she passed, we all felt the loss but everyone was richer for having known her.

Mom was incredibly empathetic, but she did not cry with people, she strengthened them. Mom did not pity people. Even while faced with huge obstacles, she showed through her dignity and perseverance what people could do with their lives. Mom not only loved her children, she also believed in them. I remember, a number of times, when I was very young, finding myself in trouble in the principal's office or in trouble with a neighbor. Mom always came to my defense, trying to find out the root of my behavior and letting me know, I could do better. She didn't tell us what to do; she showed us what to do. She expected us to act like *Menshen* and showed us how.

Mom wasn't a great writer, she wasn't a great mathematician. However, she was a great teacher. She taught us by example. She taught us how to live. She believed in honesty, self-respect and respect for others. She believed in standing straight and walking straight both literally and figuratively. She believed family and friends come first. If you have this and your health you have everything. If we have learned a fraction of what Mom has so patiently taught us all, we too can be successful. Mom wanted to be remembered dancing. We will all do her honor. We will remember how beautifully she danced through her life. Mom was truly a woman of valor.

Nancy's Words:

I have been twice blessed. When I fell in love with Stewart at sixteen, I also fell in love with Sara and Dov. They have been mother and father to me after I lost my parents, and I loved them with that same heartfelt love I had for my own mother and father. Sara was my Ima, and she and I would say how lucky we were that we ended up together. She taught me so much about life and love.

She had a way of making each of us feel how special we were in her life and her motherly devotion was endearing. She would call to remind us to dress warmly on a cold day and to get a flu shot in early October. She would call with the latest foods to eat or stop eating for our good health, and we'd laugh about what might be recommended next. We talked about philosophy, religion, and literature. We worried about the state of world affairs and weren't beyond a little gossip now and again. We *quelled* over her grandchildren as only a mother and grandmother can.

She was our biggest fan. We could do no wrong. She saved all the children's drawings, tests, stories and even my newspaper columns. I must say that even at the age of 53, I loved that someone out there cared enough to want to re-read something I wrote.

Then there was the food. It was delicious and plentiful and arrived in Tupperware containers regularly on the train. For the bigger holiday feasts she'd arrive with suitcases full of everything from chopped liver to brisket to sweet potatoes to three different kinds of cakes and cookies. She fed not only us, but also our friends and neighbors. There was always enough food for each of us to take home goodie-bags to enjoy for days after.

We just had to tell her one of us had a sore throat, and the pot of soup would be simmering on her stove before the phone conversation ended. Even when we changed out diets: eating more protein and less fat, eating no meat, eating eggs but no fish, eating veggies and tofu, but only if the tofu was carefully disguised – she creatively came up with recipes to please each of us – introducing late in life her famous veggies burger which had the meat lovers pushing the vegetarians out of the way to get at them.

She genuinely loved to be with people, to hear their stories, and she always told her own story. It was very important to her that people know about the Holocaust, about what was done. She suffered terribly throughout the years from what she experienced and witnessed during that dark time. She was haunted by it, but not undermined. She held her head high and carried herself elegantly and showed the world that she not only survived, but triumphed. She could have come out of those experiences an angry and bitter woman – but instead she was all about love. She loved with a full heart and told each of us, at the end of every conversation that she loved us. Even in her last days, her I love you message was spoken with the little energy she had left.

I miss her tremendously already. But I know her special strength is in me too and she will inspire me the rest of my days. I am a better person for having had the privilege of sharing her life and she will always have my gratitude, respect, and love. I do not say good-by today to my Ima, but *L'Hitraot* – See you later – because I believe that this amazing, difficult, beautiful, sorrowful rollercoaster of emotions and experiences that are our lives is just a prelude to an eternal life which we will share.

So Imale, Thank you for all you've been to me, and *L'Hitraot.*

Rita's Words:

"Where there's life – there's hope" is the mantra by which I will always remember my Aunt Sara. Knowing this day has come does not make the writing of this letter any easier – for you to read or for me to write.

To tell you how very sorry I am for the loss of your loving, caring, and loyal wife, mother, and grandmother, mother-in-law, and confidant is insufficient. To tell you how very sorry I am for the loss of a beautiful, intelligent, and gracious woman is inadequate. But dwelling and reflecting upon her loss is something that needs to be done before looking toward next week, next month, and next year. During these difficult days ahead, please know that your loss and grief is shared by so many people. She and all of you will be in the thoughts, hearts, and prayers of all who know her – near and far.

Aunt Sara touched so many people in so many ways with her kindnesses, her encouraging words, her attentiveness, her generosity, her courage, and optimism. That is how I will always remember her; and for that, I will always be grateful.

I wish I had been there for her and for all of you in a more significant and meaningful way. But, looking at past transgressions is not always useful. Our disparate, busy, and selfish lives pull us apart and make us lose sight of what's important. Family is important – and I'm glad I'm part of yours.

To all of you, my deepest sympathies and may your hearts heal quickly.

The following, from dear friends and family, are a selection of hundreds of condolence emails and letters that the family received:

"Life is not just taken away, but transformed.
But sad though the shade of the death may be, we must remember that we were not created for this world but
for the eternity."
We would like to express our deep sadness to the family, for the death of Mrs. Paul, taking to you our hug of solidarity at this difficult and bitter moment.

Receive our feelings,
Director of Famossul and employees, Brazil

In these times words are useless… We just want with this message to show our feelings and regret for the death of such a lovely person… We are sure that she is illuminated by the Divine Light and that she already found its flowery corner in much peace… At this difficult moment through which you are passing, we would like to offer a friendly shoulder, an embrace and some comfort. It's all we can do now. Please know that we will always be here ready to receive you with open arms with kindness and affection.
Moveis America Family

Dear Mr. Paul, Stewart, and Gil,
I am very sorry to hear about the death of Mrs. Paul.
It's indeed very sad. I am sure we all lost a very special person,
as I know she did so much for so many people.
In these 29 years working with you, I met Mrs. Paul 4-5 times but
it seems to me that I knew her for all my life.   It's a real loss to
me that she is now gone.
My heart goes out to you all, and I wish I could
attend her memorial.
My sympathies to you all. Stay with God!!

Best,
Elza, San Paulo, Brazil

Dear Ernest,
It was sad to hear from Tony that your wife Sarah passed away. She was always
very friendly to us, when we met her during the Frankfurt Fair or in New York.
She took care of us and it was a pleasure to talk to her. Her heart was open and
she was always close to Israel and her religion. We have been in Israel last time in
2005 meeting rowing friends and so we feel always very close to this country and
our friends.
Please give my condolences to Stewart and Gil.

Rudi Schader and Marion, Frankfurt, Germany

Dear Mr. Paul, Stewart, Gil, Steve,
I sympathize with you on the loss of you wife, mother, and aunt
to whom I know you were all deeply devoted, as she was to you.
Words aren't much comfort at this time, but I'd like you to know
that I've had a heavy heart since receiving the sad news. It was
a privilege to have met Mrs. Paul and I know from her warmth
and strength that her loss will be felt by many, for a long time
to come. Being a child and grandchild of Holocaust survivors
myself, I have the utmost admiration and respect for Mrs. Paul.
Rami joins me in sending affection and deepest sympathy to you
and your family. Please call on us if there is anything
we can do.

Affectionately,
Ilene & Rami Elbaz, Tel Aviv, Israel

Hi Stewart,

Jay passed along your email regarding your mom's health. I will always remember
Sara Paul as strong, caring, beautiful and stylish with so much heart and such a
strong character. She made us all feel like we were the most important people in
the room.
My prayers are with you and your family. Please extend my love to your father. He
is very special to me.

Regards,
Jim

Dearest Ernest, Dahlia, Stuart, Gil and families,

Just read about Sara, such a sad morning.

When I think about Sara and her life — she truly was a tribute to the world. I consider myself one of the true fortunate people to have known her and to have been a part of her life. There was nothing she could not do. She was so beautiful, such a fashion plate... and man, oh man, what a cook and hostess.

When I moved to Biddle Road — she was my mentor. She taught me everything... I didn't know anyone and she was my mother, my mother and my best friend. We did everything together. She taught me about acrylic nails... Dr. Orenshreik and silicone... and Edyth's. I became part of Philadelphia, missing Long Island every day of my life. But she changed that... she showed me that Philadelphia could fill the same need and that New York was only two hours away.

I cannot imagine what life would be like without Chicken Paprikash and chocolate rum balls. Every time I make it — not that it tastes one bit like Sara's — I smile to myself thinking about how many kreplach she made me throw away because my corners weren't good enough.

I bought in Margate Towers because of her — she introduced me to the shore — I only knew about Coney Island and Manhattan Beach in Brooklyn. The first time I saw the Ocean Club was with Sara... and look how that turned out. I followed her everywhere.

She was so proud of all of you... her family was the best, smartest and everything to her. She always said — "Look what happened. From two people we have a tribe." Her best line of advice — and I repeat it to everyone all the time — "When you became a mother-in-law you keep your mouth shut and your pocketbook open." She was one of the rarities in life — she loved her daughters-in-law from the moment she met them. She was so happy with her children, grandchildren, and great-grandchildren.

When she spoke about the babies – she was on fire with passion and love. But Ernest was her heart and soul. We spent hours talking about the war, before the ware and after… and it was always about Ernest. He was her lifeline from the day he walked into the kibbutz.

I was lucky enough to be accepted into her circle of friends – the bungalow group. We played cards, talked, and a new world was opened up for me. I never realized the intensity of the "New Americans" nor did I realize the hostilities they had to face. I learned about the bigotry and the isolation. I was ready to fight the world – but they were so strong – they could face anything – and they did not need me to fight their battles… just to understand and accept… and I certainly did.

I really think that my relationship with Sara and Ernest and the history that they had influenced my seeking out a Jewish institution and working for the Jewish Museum in Philadelphia. I started in 1980 and am still there… they instilled a sense of responsibility and love for Israel and Judaism.

I don't want to turn this letter into the next great American novel. I just want to tell you how lucky I was to know Sara Paul and how important she was to my life and that I will always miss her.

She deserves a big Celebration of Life – because she loved life and enjoyed it to the hilt.

Stan, Cari, Alysa and I will always think of her with admiration and respect. SHE WAS SOME LADY.

All our love and condolences are with you.

Elaine Silverman, Philadelphia

Stewart,

Thanks so much for sharing your wife's incredible words about your mother. Please tell her how moved I was to learn even more than I knew about a most remarkable woman. I knew that she was a fantastic wife, mother, friend and so dedicated to her family--but I loved learning more about her close group of friends and her dedication to Israel, helping all children, and her passion for our great country as a "New American." She was truly amazing and Nancy did her, Ernie, you and your whole family very proud. She has a gift with words!

Please give my very best Passover greetings to you wonderful father. I think of him very often and know how much he must miss your mother, but you must remind him how she made sure he would never be alone by giving him her special children, their spouses, grandchildren and great-grandchildren. They were a remarkable couple, and I pray for him to live a healthy and fulfilling life going forward, in her memory and honor.

Best regards,
Marvin, Fort Worth, Texas

Dear Ernest:

Today I was on my way back from Santo Domingo, when I received a phone call from María Eugenia Lanas informing me on Sara's death.

I was shocked to say the least. It is true that I did not have recent news from you but as the saying says, "No news, good news." I was hoping that both you and Sara were in good health and maybe enjoying the holidays you always had during this time of the year. Destiny is cruel sometimes and this time it was your turn. I deeply regret that a very splendid friend such as you is now suffering the loss of his wife.

Ernest, my deepest sympathies with all my heart. I will always remember Sara and hope the good Lord will help mitigate your pain.

A big hug from
Patricio & Ana María, San Diego, Chile

My Dear Ernie and Stewart,

I am heartbroken that we no longer have Sara Paul on this earth. Sara always brought a sense of stability and well being to me. She always had wonderful pearls of wisdom to share with me.

I had not seen Sara in a large number of years but my memories of her are clear and vivid. I will always remember her vibrancy.

Please accept my most heartfelt condolences and most sincere prayers for Sara, for you and for all of your family.

I am currently traveling abroad and am in China right now. I will not return to the US until the end of the month.

Most Sincerely,
Jim Prucha

Dear Stewart and Family,

We know how difficult it is when we have to face the pain of losing somebody who is part of the family. We'll pray for you to find in God your great consolation for this Mourning and Crying days because nobody can help better than He. May faith bring comfort to all of you at this time of deep sorrow.

We know that words are useless in these hours but our thoughts are with you and your family in these difficult times. Feel hugged by all of your Brazilian friends at Planor.

Luis & Anete, Rafael & Soraia, Bubi & Dilma,
Vilmar, Ramón, Neiva
Lucilene, Ester, Krüger, Cristiano, Daniel K, Alceu, Erivelton
Sao Bento, Santa Catarina, Brazil

Dear Stewart,

I have heard from Anete of your dear mother's passing away.

In my mind's eye I shall always see her as the positive, energetic lady we all saw at Luis and Anete's anniversary in Sept 1999 and at Rafael & Soraia's wedding. I am sure that all the fond memories of your mother will stay with you and your whole family for all the years to come.

To you, to our dearest Mr. Paul, and to the whole Family I extend my condolences and deep sympathy.

Lots of love,
Simone Regina, Sao Bento, Santa Catarina, Brazil

Stewart,

I would like to let you know how shocked and heartbroken I am about the tragedy of the death of Mrs. Sarah Paul that hit the Paul (and Primex family) at one of its most sensitive points. My condolences go first to you and your brothers and sisters who have lost your lovely mother. I wish also to express my sympathy and my solidarity with your father.

Primex has been my second home for almost 15 years and my ties with you are those of an intense partnership, even of friendship, that has grown over the years of joint efforts in promoting the Brazilian business.

May the God Spirit - The Lord of Our Lives - be your strength.

Hugs,
Ramón, Sao Bento, Santa Catarina, Brazil

Stewart,

Words can't say what we are feeling. We will remember her for the rest of our lives. Your family is an example to us and we pray for you all everyday.

May God bless you and all the Paul family.

Love,
Rafa and Family, Sao Bento, Santa Catarina, Brazil

Dear Stewart, Dear Gil,

We are very saddened to hear of the passing of your mother. I know that at such times, it is very difficult to find consolation.

A few years ago I had the honor of spending a whole day with your parents in Israel. I was impressed by the noble woman your mother was—to see how she cared about people, even people she met only a few hours before.

Please accept our deepest condolences for your loss. Please convey my sincere condolences to your father.

May the Lord grant you and your family strength. I wish all of you will know no more sorrow.

Sincerely,

Ilan Mali and Family, Tel Aviv, Israel

Dear Stewart and Gil:

Although we've known for a long time that your mom was making a courageous fight against an enemy that would ultimately prevail, it does not lessen in any way, the truly deep heartfelt sadness we all feel at this time.

Sara Paul was a strong, intelligent, caring, gracious lady. I consider myself very fortunate to have known her and to have had her as a friend.

Please convey my sincerest condolences to your father, Dahlia, and your families.

Ron, New York

Stewart,

I just came from the airport… Luiz told me by phone about your mother…

I have no words to tell you how sorry I am in losing another person we loved so much. She with your father was our beginning… and I'll always remember her as a strong and straightforward woman… always keeping her family
 under her wings!!!

She was so wonderful… I feel so sorry about your father… and I would like to be there to be with him, but I know that I would not be of any help since I'm broken hearted. Please give him a very warm hug and tell him that it is me hugging him …

I will never forget your Mom's mourning days, as on Sunday (Jan 20th) we used to celebrate Danny's birthday, and now… it is hard and painful, but we have to go on and try to survive. Stewart, your mother is with Danny in another much better place where only fortunate people can be… my hope is to be there sometime… and I'm sure that we'll meet each other again, forever…

Please hug all your beloved family… Nancy, your kids, Gil, his wife and Dahlia … and all who know me… I'm very sorry…

Stewart, God be with you in your grief… Today is difficult and the next days will be even worst… be prepared to feel emptiness and sadness in the days to come, because you lost a very dear friend who was there all the time you needed her and also on other occasions when you just wanted to have somebody to talk to… She was part of yourself, as your father is and her absence will hurt so
much in your soul…

From the bottom of my heart, I'm very, very sorry…

With love to all of you, especially Mr. Ernest Paul,
Anete, Sao Bento, Santa Catarina, Brazil

A Tree Will Be Planted In Memory Of

SARAH PAUL

A Wonderful Woman, Who Graced Us All With Her Presence

Planted With Love By

Bonnie & Sam Perilstein

In the memorial forest for the 1.5 million children who died in the Holocaust

שרה שלנו איננה
למרות שידענו שזה כה צפוי
נדהמנו לשמוע שזה בא.
שרה שלנו את כולנו עזבה
אשת חיל, עוגן המשפחה
השאירה את כולנו שבורי לב ומתגעגעים.
רוצה אני לכתוב כמה מילים
בשם כל משפחת ארגוב,
אנחנו כבר בחסרונה מרגישים.
תמיד ידעה לשמור על קשר חם וקרוב,
גם שהיינו רחוקים גאוגרפית,
ידענו ששרה איתנו בשמחה ובעצב בבריאות ובחולי.
כשנפרדנו ביולי עדיין קיוותה שבחורף תבוא לבקר את המשפחה.
לכולם דאגה ואת המשפחה איחדה.
אנו מבקשים מכם משפחת פול הנרחבת,
שתזכרו שגם אתכם אוהבים כאן ורוצים לשמור על קשר.
מבכים את מותה, אך דבריה המעודדים:
"בכל מקום שיש חיים יש גם תקווה" ילוו אותנו גם בעתיד.
שמרו על דב ועל המשפחה היפה והחמה ששרה טיפחה.

אוהבים משפחת ארגוב.

Our Sara is gone.
Although we knew it's unavoidable
We were stunned when it came.
Our Sara left us all
Eshet Chaiyl, the anchor of the family
She left us all, heartbroken, missing her.
I would like to write some words
In the name of the Argov family,
We already feel her absence.
She always knew to maintain a close and warm relationship,
Even though we were geographically apart,
Sara has always been with us in happiness or sorrow, health or
sickness.
In July when we said goodbye, she still had hope that in the winter
she'll come to Israel to visit the family.
She cared about everyone and united the family.
We ask all of you, the wide Paul family;
Remember that, we love you very much and want to keep in touch.
We are weeping Sara's death and forever embrace her reassuring
words:
"Where there is life there is hope".
Take care of Dov and the beautiful warm family Sara nurtured.

Love, the Argov family

Sara Triumphant!

Sara's favorite poem captures Sara's sweet spirit and
how she would want her dear family to feel about her death:

Do not stand at my grave and weep,
I am not there, I do not sleep.

I am a thousand winds that blow.
I am the diamond glint on snow.
I am the sunlight on ripened grain.
I am the gentle autumn rain.

When you wake in the morning hush,
I am the swift, uplifting rush
Of quiet birds in circling flight.
I am the soft starlight at night.

Do not stand at my grave and weep.
I am not there, I do not sleep.
Do not stand at my grave and cry.
I am not there, I did not die!

Do not stand at my grave and weep.
I am not there, I do not sleep.

I am the song that will never end.
I am the love of family and friend.
I am the child who has come to rest
In the arms of the Father who knows him best.

When you see the sunset fair,
I am the scented evening air.
I am the joy of a task well done.
I am the glow of the setting sun.

Do not stand at my grave and weep.
I am not there, I do not sleep.
Do not stand at my grave and cry.
I am not there, I did not die!

—Mary E. Frye

⬧ Chapter 29 ⬧

Friends

Sara Paul, Lili Herskovich, and Rachel Ickovich—these three good friends had one and the same destiny. In December 2006, Sara was the first one to be diagnosed with cancer. Rachel was diagnosed in early 2007; Lili, in February 2008.

Friendship among the three of them, all Holocaust survivors, had a beginning in Haifa, Israel, in the early 1950s. They all lived near each other; their friendship continued and grew stronger and stronger for over fifty years. Only death parted them.

The strongest common denominator among them was their children: Rachel's three children, Ely, Tova, and Jeanette; Lili, two wonderful sons, Michael and Howard; Sara with three extraordinary, loving, caring children: Dahlia, Stewart, and Gil. May G-d bless all the children.

The age differences among the kids were only a year or two. Many weekends were planned together among the families. During the winter was sleigh riding in Pennypacker Park; summers in sunny Atlantic City. The beach was a playground for the kids— digging in the warm sand and running to the ocean.

Philadelphia, 1957: Sister in law, Manci, Sara, and my sister, Chaja

At one point we had over ten children to watch out for— all for one; the three moms were there with their watchful eyes. During many years we all rented rooms in the same house, Marika's, on Dover and Atlantic Avenues, one block from the ocean. The kids mingled, playing happily.

My sister-in-law, Manci, was the link to Marika for they were the best of friends. Manci was the first to arrive in Atlantic City with her two kids, Miriam and Steve. As my brother Villi had a business to run in Philadelphia, he came mostly for long weekends, which was the experience of all the husbands. As Manci was the senior (the oldest) among us, she took charge of the kitchen, allocating kitchen time for the others. Often she even told the others what to cook and how to cook it. She was known to love to taste everyone's food. She was a great cook and had a good heart to share with everyone. Manci had a special soft spot for Sara. Their close relationship was remarkable.

Guests from year to year used to come down every summer— most were survivors. There were the Pauls: my brother Emil, Lili, and their three, Rifka, David, Nir; Rachel and Barry Ickovich with their three; Sara and Zali-Ben Ami and their son, Moishe; Frida and Moske Davidovitch with daughter Chanele; Sara and Josef Katz with daughter, Rifkele, and son, David; and Fruma and Jo Fridman with daughter Billa and son Ira.

At the beach we all sat together. We often shared fruit and lunches, and of course we had ice cream for the kids and some adults as well.

The women cooked up a storm in the one kitchen shared by all. Before sunset, we came back to a house scented by the various dishes cooking and baking—many Hungarian specialties.

When the children were back in the house, there was never a dull moment. One, two, or three cried; they had some sunburn. All the mothers were there with their remedies.

After showers and early dinners, everyone got ready to go for the daily parade on the boardwalk. The evening walks on the famous boardwalk were always challenging. The kids were running for the ice cream store, followed shortly by the visit to Roth's candy store.

The women dressed elegantly. The husbands always knew the difference between those that were staring at our beautiful children or our beautiful wives. Shimi, Lili's husband (passed away in 2006), Barry, Rachel's husband, and Ernest, Sara's husband always walked behind them or before them carrying the smallest of the children.

As we looked at all the children, we were remembering that despite Hitler and the Nazis, what a future generation we have!

Around 8:00 PM everyone was back at the house. The kids were put to bed one by one. For the adults card playing was the past time, and cards they played! During the winter we continued to meet every weekend—each family took turns to host the card games.

A friendly family atmosphere always prevailed; the snacks and particularly the Hungarian special pastries were the "icing on the cake." The wives cooked basically the same wonderful dishes and baked the same delicious cakes. At some point, Sara, Rachel, Lily, Frida and

Manci matched the color of their hair. Ernest says, "I think this was a statement of real deep friendship and identity."

There were few days during the years that the five did not phone each other. There was always something to say, always something to share. At the end, the illness of each affected the others.

Manci passed away first. In 2008, Sara passed away; four months later, Lili, followed by Rachel five months later—all in one year. Their common suffering impacted each other. May their good memories be celebrated forever.

Only Frida of the five has survived. She and her husband, Moshke, live in Philadelphia; their daughter, Dr. Helen Ehannele and her husband, David, in Pittsburgh.

Sara, Rachel and Lili are resting near each other in the King David Cemetery in Bensalem, Pennsylvania. Manci is resting close by.

&.. Chapter 30 ..&

Mom-Mom, Our Hero

The following was written by Tara, Sara's granddaughter, on behalf of her sister, Ilana, and herself. It seems fitting to end Sara's memoir with the words of Sara's grandchildren, the continuing generations—Sara's triumph over the evil of the Shoah.

From the moment you met my grandmother, Sara Paul, you were drawn in. She made people feel that they were special and loved and cared for.

As her first-born grandchildren, my sister, Ilana, and I developed a very special and unique bond with our grandmother right from the beginning. We have shared many memories and very special times together. She helped to raise us, always saying her home was our second home and that she was our second mother. Spending time at her house meant baking cookies, dance recitals, bowling, and shopping. Our summers were spent in Atlantic City, in a small one bedroom apartment. Mom-Mom and Saba took us on the amusement rides, the beach, wherever we wanted to go. Mom-Mom never missed our first days of school, dance recitals, visiting days at camp, weddings, or the births of her great-grandchildren.

Through the years, Mom-Mom went beyond what the average grandmother would do. For instance, we traveled with her to Europe and Israel. This experience will never be forgotten.

I'd have to say, though, my favorite and most cherished time spent with Mom-Mom was when we spent time alone talking. I would visit her in New York. We would go see a Broadway show, have dinner, and then get into bed and talk . . . for hours. She would share her past with me: the hardship she and her family endured. I lived for those moments . . . they were special, but also heartbreaking.

I have made a commitment, not only to honor my grandmother's memory, but also to myself as an educator, and as a thank you to her, to teach my students about the Holocaust. I will teach my students and my own children to be kind to one another. I will teach them about peace, friendship, and respect. I will teach them about the evils of prejudice, bullying, and discrimination. I will teach them to accept differences in other people and inform them about what can happen if they don't. I will teach them not to judge others and to defend those that may need help.

Mom-Mom will forever be in our memories and hearts. She will live on through all of us. She will forever be missed and loved.

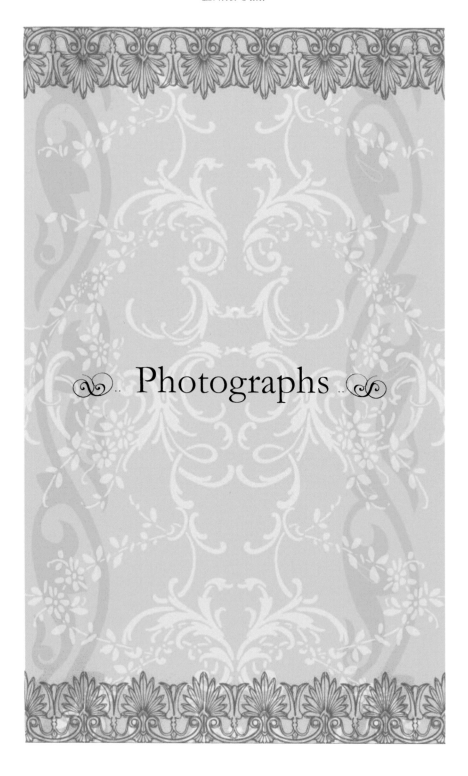

Photographs

Israel, 1949, Sara

Israel, 1949, Ernest in Israeli military

Tivon, Israel, 1951: L to R Lili, Rifka, Emil, Sara, Dahlia, Ernest, Chaja, Avraham, Shalom

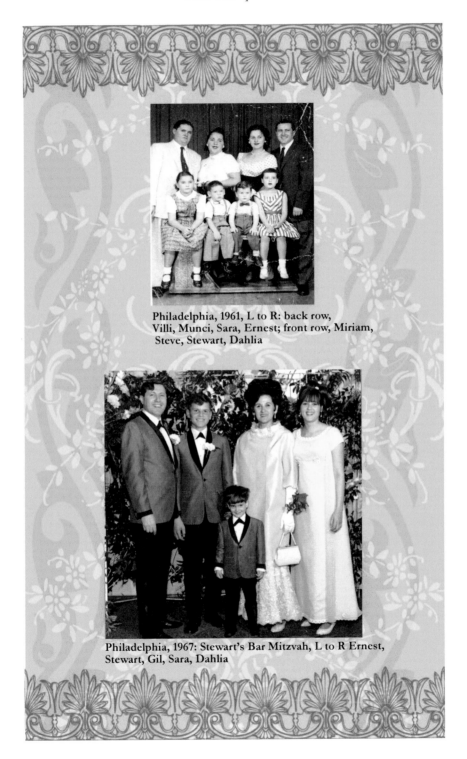

Philadelphia, 1961, L to R: back row,
Villi, Munci, Sara, Ernest; front row, Miriam,
Steve, Stewart, Dahlia

Philadelphia, 1967: Stewart's Bar Mitzvah, L to R Ernest,
Stewart, Gil, Sara, Dahlia

Philadelphia, 1970: Bernie (Nancy's father), Sara, Buba Chava,
Ernest, Nancy, Edith (Nancy's mother)

Philadelphia, June 2, 1974:
Nancy and Stewart's Wedding

Budapest, Hungary,1980:
Sara, overlooking the capitol building

Budapest, Hungary, 1980:
Sara, at Ernest's father's tombstone

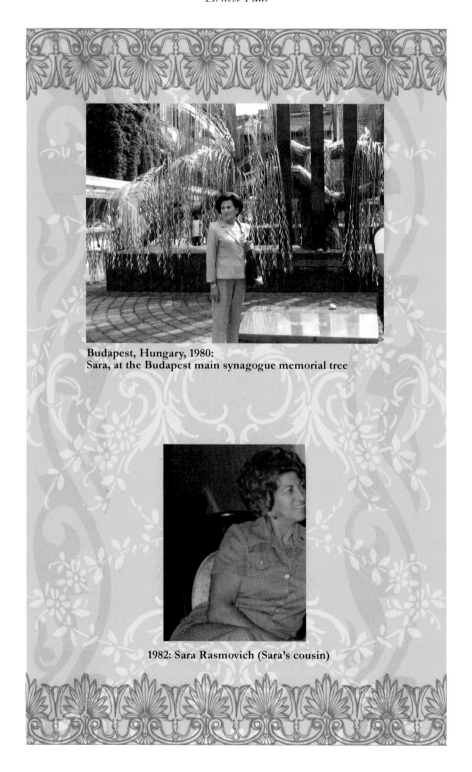

Budapest, Hungary, 1980:
Sara, at the Budapest main synagogue memorial tree

1982: Sara Rasmovich (Sara's cousin)

Israel, 1982: Adi's Bar Mitzvah, L to R Zipi, Gil, Shalom, Anat,
Adi (Ronnie and Zipi's son, our nephew), Chaja, Ronnie, Stewart, Sara, Ernest

Lebanon, 1984: Stewart

Israel, 1985: L to R Ernest, Yocheved (Eva), Sara, Zvi

Gan Yasmine, Israel, July 3, 1990:
Dali and Gil's Wedding

Gan Yasmine, Israel, July 3, 1990:
Friends of Sara and Ernest at Dali and Gil's Wedding

Atlantic City, July 15, 1995: 50th Wedding Anniversary,
Sara and Ernest

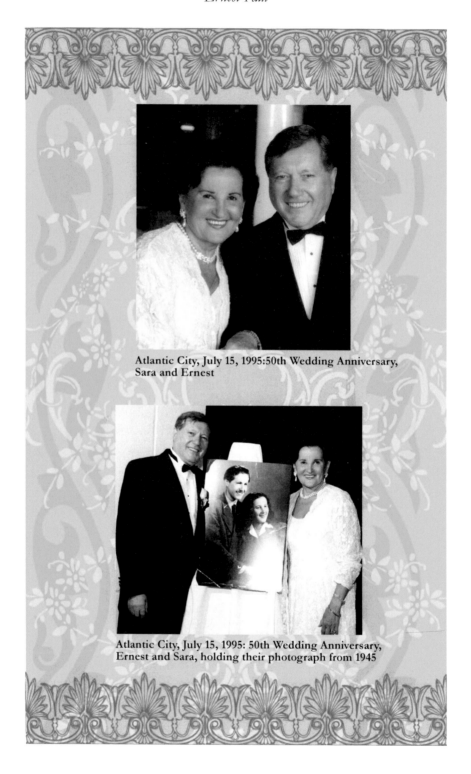

Atlantic City, July 15, 1995:50th Wedding Anniversary, Sara and Ernest

Atlantic City, July 15, 1995: 50th Wedding Anniversary, Ernest and Sara, holding their photograph from 1945

Atlantic City, July 15, 1995: 50th Wedding Anniversary, Sara and Ernest

Atlantic City, July 15, 1995: 50th Wedding Anniversary, The Paul children—L to R Stewart, Dahlia, Gil

Atlantic City, July 15, 1995:
50th Wedding Anniversary, Ernest and Sara

Atlantic City, July 15, 1995: 50th Wedding Anniversary, The Paul Family

Atlantic City, July 15, 1995: 50th Wedding Anniversary, Grandchildren: L to R: Tara, Eitan, Elite, Ari, and Ilana, with Ernest and Sara

Atlantic City, July 15, 1995: 50th Wedding Anniversary, L to R Stewart, Eitan, Nancy, Ari

Atlantic City, July 15, 1995: 50th Wedding Anniversary, Gil, Elite, Dali

Crystal Line Cruise, December 1995: Sara and Ernest

Atlantic City, July 15, 1995: 50th Wedding Anniversary,
L to R Joyce, Steve P, Chaja, Ernest, Sara, Christian, Juan Eduardo

1996: L to R Ilana, Dahlia, Sara, and Tara

Hyatt, Princeton, NJ, 2003: Eitan's Bar Mitzvah,
L to R Ari, Ernest, Eitan, Sara, Nancy, Stewart

Neve Shalom, Metuchen, NJ, December 20, 2008:
Daniel's Bar Mitzvah, L to R Gil, Elite, Daniel, Dali, Ernest

Neve Shalom, Metuchen, NJ, December 20, 2008:
Daniel's Bar Mitzvah, L to R Gil, Daniel, Ernest

Neve Shalom, Metuchen, NJ, December 20, 2008:
Daniel's Bar Mitzvah, Family

Neve Shalom, Metuchen, NJ, December 20, 2008:
Daniel's Bar Mitzvah, Family

Stev and Dahila, 2008

2008: Our great-grandchildren:
Top row, Roman and Jaky; Second, Shony; Third, Ry-Ry Sara and Cole

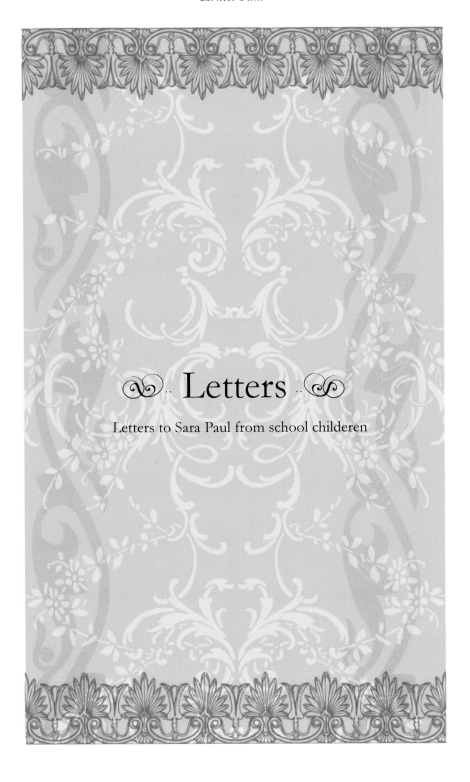

Letters

Letters to Sara Paul from school childeren

Dear Mrs. Paul,

Today was very special to me. I am so interested in your stories. I will keep your story in my heart forever and I just want you to know you are a very brave woman to have survived such a horrible time of the Holocaust. Thankyou for coming to are school it was a privalige.

Sincerely,

Hiathy Beeston

(Mrs. Cooler)

6/6/01

Dear Mrs. Paul,

Thank you for coming and telling me the most hardest time of your life when you said how they treated you I almost started to cry just because your diffient from them they want to hert you. I don't know how they can hert someone so nice and beutiful. And I want to say sorry for what you had to go through and to take care of yourself and the people you love the most in you life.

Love
Tina Ritz.

Dear Mrs. Paul,

I'm realy sorry about your relatives. I know how you feel! Thanks you sharing your memories with us. I know if I went to concentration camp would died immediately so I wouldn't have to deal with any violence. I will try to remember your story and will remember

You!!

P.S. I'm glad you didn't die because I like mrs. Pomerantz!!

Love,
Alex Beer

Dear Mrs. Paul,

I wont to thanks forcomeing to my School and telling your story. I had never heard any thing so alful in my life. I dont think I will ever forget it. I am glad that you did Survive, So I could learn about it in a differnt way. My Social Studies books only gives a litte paragraph on the topic and it was Such a big issue!

Thankyou again

Kaitlynn Yager

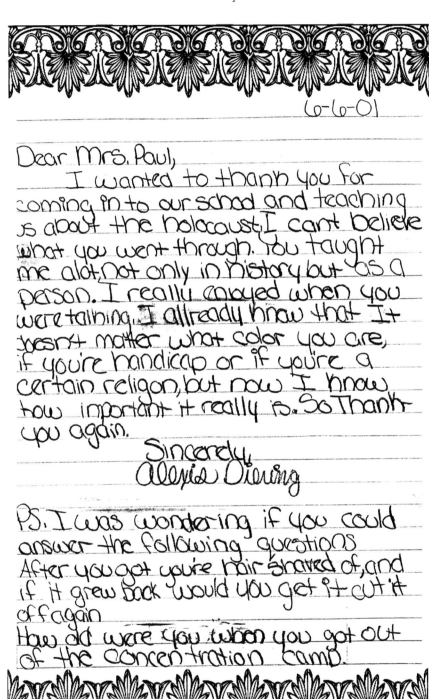

6-6-01

Dear Mrs. Paul,

  I wanted to thank you for coming into our school and teaching us about the holocaust, I cant beliee what you went through. You taught me alot, not only in history but as a person. I really enjoyed when you were talking. I allready know that It doesn't matter what color you are, if you're handicap or if you're a certain religon, but now I know how important it really is. So Thank you again.

     Sincerely,
    Alexia Diering

P.S. I was wondering if you could answer the following questions
After you got you're hair shaved of, and if it grew back would you get it cut it off again
How old were you when you got out of the concentration camp.

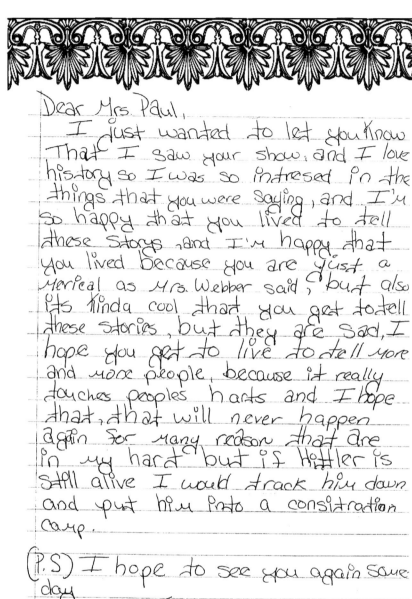

Dear Mrs. Paul,

I just wanted to let you know That I saw your show, and I love history so I was so intresed in the things that you were saying, and I'm so happy that you lived to tell these Storys, and I'm happy that you lived because you are yust a merical as Mrs. Webber said, but also its kinda cool that you get to tell these stories, but they are sad, I hope you get to live to tell more and more people, because it really touches peoples harts and I hope that, that will never happen again for many reason that are in my hart but if Hittler is still alive I would track him down and put him into a consitration camp.

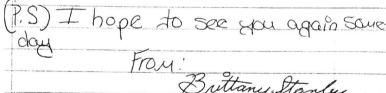

(P.S) I hope to see you again some day

From:

Brittany Stanley

Dear Mrs. Paul,

Thank you for sharing with me your experiances. I'm so sorry that a pearson as nice as you are had to suffer like that. I really injoyed you telling me about what you had to go through. I really did learn a lesson about being kind to one another. You are really a strong and brave pearson to survive the holocaust. I dont think it is right that just because you are a Jew you should be punished. Thank you again.

Yours truly,
Amanda Evans

Jordan Fisher

Dear Mrs. Paul,

I want to thank you for coming down from New York all the way to New Jersey. To tell us about the havlocuast and why it was so bad. Now that we know that, we will make sure it does not happen ~~agian~~ again. We will be nice to others and not cruel to others because like I said we do not ~~wont~~ want that to happen again and it wouln't.

I have a question why did they kill poor little babys when they didn't even do anything?

20 Essex Ave.
Erial, NJ 08081
May 3, 1999

Dear Mrs. Paul,

Thank you so much for coming in last Friday. It was so interesting, I now know a lot more about the Holocaust. That one part about the baby being smacked against the pole I was about to cryyyyy! Why didn't the Nazis just kill Hitler, they were the one's with the guns. The Nazis are monsters and Dr. Mengela "the Angel of Death" is actually the "DEVIL OF DEATH"!! Thank you so much so much for coming in I really appreciate it.

Sincerely,
Bobby
Wagner

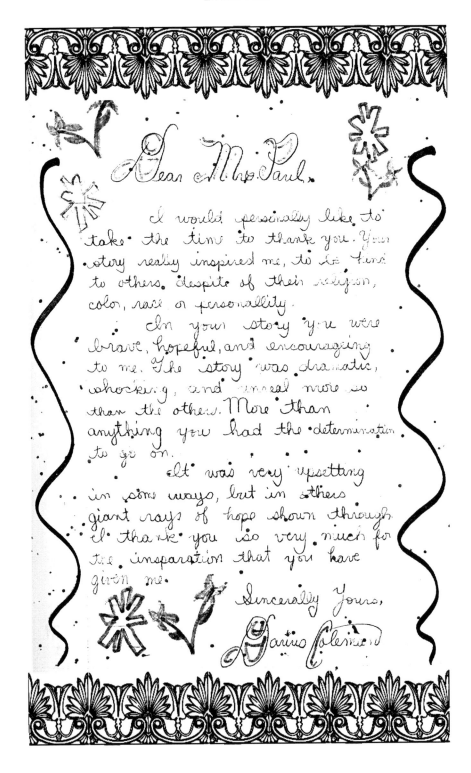

Dear Mrs. Paul,

I would personally like to take the time to thank you. Your story really inspired me, to be kind to others despite of their religion, color, race or personality.

In your story you were brave, hopeful, and encouraging to me. The story was dramatic, shocking, and unreal more so than the others. More than anything you had the determination to go on.

It was very upsetting in some ways, but in others giant rays of hope shown through. I thank you so very much for the insparation that you have given me.

Sincerally Yours,

Darius Coleman

Endnotes

[1] **Tisa River**, also Tisza River, tributary of the Danube River, one of the major rivers of Central Europe, marks Slovak-Hungarian border.

[2] **Rabbi Baal Shem Tov**, or Rabbi Yisrael ben Eliezer (1698-1760), founder an important religious movement in Jewish history, *Chassidus* (Hasidic Movement). **After his marriage, Rabbi Yisrael and his wife moved to a small town in the Carpathian Mountains (possibly Krivé).** When he died, he left behind a movement that continued to be significant force in the Jewish world. "Rabbi Baal Shem Tov." Jewish Virtual Library. Web 27 Apr. 2010.

[3] *Chuppah* (or *Huppah*) In Judaism, the canopy under which a marriage ceremony is conducted. "Chuppah." Jewish Virtual Library, Glossary. Web. 27 Apr. 2010.

[4] **Diamond cutting** Sara's father would have gone to Antwerp to learn his profession. "The earliest diamond-cutting industry is believed to have been in Venice, a trade capital, starting sometime after 1330. Diamond cutting may have arrived in Paris by the late 14th century; in Bruges—on the diamond trade route—there is documentation for the technique in 1465." "Diamond Cutting." American Museum of Natural History. Web 27 Apr. 2010.

"Over the centuries Antwerp, Belgium, became the diamond cutting capital. Since the 15th Century Antwerp has played an important role in the diamond trade and industry 'Antwerp quality' and 'Antwerp cut' are international trade terms synonymous with perfect processing and flawless beauty." "Diamonds." Antwerp. Web 27 Apr. 2010.

[5] **Gramophone** "On November 8 1887, Emile Berliner, a German immigrant working in Washington D.C., patented a successful system of sound recording. Berliner was the first inventor to stop recording on cylinders and start recording on flat disks or records.

The first records were made of glass, later zinc, and eventually plastic. A spiral groove with sound information was etched into the flat record. The record was rotated on the gramophone. The 'arm' of the gramophone held a needle that read the grooves in the record by vibration and transmitting the information to the gramophone speaker. "Gramaphone." Inventors. Web. 27 Apr. 2010.

[6] **Passover (Pesach)** "The major Jewish spring holiday (with agricultural aspects) also known as *hag hamatzot* (festival of unleavened bread), commemorating the Exodus or deliverance of the Hebrew people from Egypt (see Exodus 12-13). The festival lasts eight days, during which Jews refrain from eating all leavened foods and products. A special ritual meal called the *Seder* is prepared, and a traditional narrative called the *Haggadah*, supplemented by hymns and songs, marks the event." "Passover." Jewish Virtual Library. Web. 27 Apr. 2010.

[7] **Hanukkah** ("Festival of Lights") **"**(Heb. Dedication) Jewish festival that commemorates the rededication of the Jerusalem temple and the victory of the Maccabees over the Hellenists circa 167 BCE." "Hanukkah." Jewish Virtual Library, Glossary. Web. 27 Apr. 2010.

[8] **Orthodox Jews** "From the Greek for 'correct opinion/outlook,' as opposed to heterodox or heretical. The judgment that a position is 'orthodox' depends on what are accepted as the operative 'rules' or authorities at the time." "Orthodox." Jewish Virtual Library, Glossary. Web. 27 Apr. 2010.

[9] **Hasidic Jews** (Heb. Pious ones). "The term may refer to Jews in various periods: (1) a group that resisted the policies of Antiochus Epiphanes in the 2nd century B.C.E. at the start of the Maccabean revolt; (2) pietists in the 13th century; (3) followers of the Hasidic movement founded in the first half of the 18th century by Israel Baal Shem Tov." "Hasidic." Jewish Virtual Library, Glossary. Web. 27 Apr. 2010.

[10] *Yeshiva* "(also frequently referred to as a *Beth Midrash*, Talmudic Academy, Rabbinical Academy or Rabbinical School) an institution unique to classical Judaism for *Torah* study, the study of *Talmud*, Rabbinic literature and Response.

The term *yeshiva* is also used sometimes as a generic name for any school that teaches *Torah*, *Mishnah* and *Talmud*, to any age group." —wik

[11] **Torah,** *Mishnah, and Talmud*

Torah (Heb., teaching, instruction). "In general, Torah refers to study of the whole gamut of Jewish tradition or to some aspect thereof. In its special sense, the Torah refers to the 'five books of Moses' in the Hebrew scriptures (see Pentateuch). "Torah." Jewish Virtual Library, Glossary. Web. 27 Apr. 2010.

Mishnah (Heb., 'teaching') "The work is the authoritative legal tradition of the early sages and is the basis of the legal discussions of the *Talmud*." "*Mishnah*." Jewish Virtual Library, Glossary. Web. 27 Apr. 2010.

Talmud (Heb., 'study" or "learning'). Rabbinic Judaism produced two *Talmuds*: the one known as the "Babylonian" is the most famous in the western world, and was completed around the fifth century CE; the other, known as the "Palestinian" or "Jerusalem" Talmud, was edited perhaps in the early fourth century CE. Both have as their common core the *Mishnah* collection of the *tannaim*, to which are added commentary and discussion (*gemara*) by the *amoraim* (teachers) of the respective locales." "*Talmud*." Jewish Virtual Library, Glossary. Web. 27 Apr. 2010.

[12] *cheder* (Heb/Yid. lit. Room) Traditional school of *Talmudic* study which draws its name from the one-room buildings in which the students studied. "*Cheder*." Jewish Virtual Library, Glossary. Web. 27 Apr. 2010.

[13] **Matzah "**crisp, flat, unleavened bread, made of flour and water, which must be baked before the dough has had time to rise. It is the only type of 'bread' that Jews may eat during Passover, and it must be made specifically for Passover use, under rabbinical supervision.

Eating Matzah on Passover (*Pesach*) commemorates the unleavened bread eaten by the Jews when they left Egypt in such haste that there was no time for the dough to rise." "Matzah." The Orthodox Union. Web. 27 Apr. 2010.

[14] *Kittel* "a white linen robe worn by Jewish men on special occasions to signify purity, holiness, and new beginnings. Traditionally, a Jewish man first wears a *kittel* on his wedding day, thereafter on Rosh Hashanah, Yom Kippur, and Passover, and ultimately as a burial shroud." "*Kittel.*" Jewish Virtual Library, Glossary. Web. 27 Apr. 2010.

[15] **Pogrom** From the Russian word for "devastation"; "an unprovoked attack or series of attacks upon a minority community, especially on Jews and Armenians." "Pogrom." Jewish Virtual Library, Glossary. Web. 27 Apr. 2010.

[16] **Kristallnacht** (Ger. "crystal night," meaning "Night of broken Glass"). Organized destruction of synagogues, Jewish houses and shops, accompanied by arrests of thousands of Jews, which took place in Germany and Austria under the Nazis on the night of Nov. 9-10, 1938.

"Kristallnacht." Jewish Virtual Library, Glossary. Web. 27 Apr. 2010.

The preferred term is The November Pogrom; the other, the German term, implies that glass was broken, but much worse happened.

[17] **Brown Shirts** "*Sturmabteilung*, abbreviated SA, (German for 'Assault detachment' or 'Assault section,' usually translated as 'stormtroop(er)s'), functioned as a paramilitary organization of the NSDAP – the German Nazi party. It played a key role in Adolf Hitler's rise to power in the 1920s and 1930s.

SA men were often called 'brownshirts,' for the color of their uniforms; this distinguished them from the *Schutzstaffel* (SS), who wore black and brown uniforms (compare the Italian blackshirts)." "Brown Shirts." Enwikipedia. Web. 27 Apr. 2010.

[18] **Eduard Benes** (1884-1951)"Benes joined with Tomas Masaryk in the fight for Czechoslovakian independence. The two men formed the Czechoslovak National Council with Benes its first general secretary. . . . As a result of the Versailles Peace Treaty the independent state of Czechoslovakia was established. Benes became foreign minister of the new country. He worked hard for the League of Nations and attempted to obtain good relations with other nations in Europe.

Benes replaced Tomas Masaryk when he retired as president in 1935. He considered the Munich Agreement negotiated by Neville Chamberlain and Adolf Hitler as a grave betrayal and resigned from office, going into voluntary exile.

In 1941 Benes became head of a Czechoslovakia provisional government in London. In March 1945 Benes flew to Moscow and along with Jan Masaryk accompanied the Russian-sponsored Czechoslovak Corps that liberated the country from Germany.

Benes remained president of Czechoslovakia for three years." After the Communist takeover in 1948, Benes resigned his office. "Eduard Benes." Spartacus. Web. 27 Apr. 2010.

[19] **Hitler and Czechoslovakia** "Although Czechoslovakia had never been part of Germany, Ethnic Germans living in Czechoslovakia liked to call themselves Germans because of their language. Most of these people lived in the Sudetenland, an area on the Czechoslovakian border with Germany.

In September 1938, Neville Chamberlain, the British prime minister, met Hitler, who threatened to invade Czechoslovakia unless Britain supported Germany's plans to takeover the Sudetenland. After discussing the issue with the Edouard Daladier (France) and Eduard Benes (Czechoslovakia), Chamberlain informed Hitler that his proposals were unacceptable.

The meeting took place in Munich on 29 September 1938. Desperate to avoid war and anxious to avoid an alliance with Joseph Stalin and the Soviet Union, Neville Chamberlain and Edouard Daladier agreed that Germany could have the Sudetenland. In return, Hitler promised not to make any further territorial demands in Europe. Adolf Hitler, Neville Chamberlain, Edouard Daladier, and Benito Mussolini signed the Munich Agreement which transferred the Sudetenland to Germany.

The German Army marched into the Sudetenland on 1 October 1938. As this area contained nearly all the country's mountain fortifications, it was no longer able to defend itself against further aggression.

By March 1939 the whole of Czechoslovakia was under the control of Germany. The Czech Army was disbanded and the Germans took control of the country's highly developed arms industry." "Sudetenland." Spartacus. Web. 27 Apr. 2010.

[20] **Jozef Tiso** (Bratislava, 13 Oct.1887; d.18 Apr.1947) Slovak; President of Slovakia 1939–1945, "Tiso was ordained as a Catholic priest in 1910. He became involved in politics after the creation of Czechoslovakia in 1918 because he resented Czech domination of the new state. Together with two other priests, Hlinka and Jehlička, he founded the Slovak People's Party, calling for Slovak autonomy. Following Hlinka's death in August 1938, Tiso became leader of the party. In October 1938 he became the premier of an autonomous Slovak government. On 14 March 1939, after the German invasion of Czechoslovakia, Tiso proclaimed Slovakia an independent republic, with himself as President. In October 1939 Slovakia became a protectorate of the Third Reich. In June 1941 Slovakia declared war on the Soviet Union, which lost Tiso support among Slovaks. He was sentenced to death by a Czechoslovak court in April 1947. The non-Communist members of Beneš's coalition government sought a reprieve, but at the insistence of the Communists. Tiso was hanged on 18 April 1947." "Jozef Tiso."

[21] **Treaty of Protection** March 23, 1939: Hitler signed the "Treaty of Protection" in Prague. He called for German control of Czech economy. "Treaty of Protection." Jewish Virtual Library. Web. 27 Apr. 2010.

[22] **WW II** (1939-1945) "a global military conflict which involved a majority of the world's nations, including all of the great powers. organized into two opposing military alliances: the Axis nations, Germany, Italy, and Japan, and the Allies: England (Great Britain, the United Kingdom), the

United States of America, the Soviet Union (U.S.S.R., Russia), and France. Other allied nations: Australia, Belgium, Bolivia, Brazil, Canada, China, Denmark, Greece, Mexico, Netherlands, New Zealand, Norway, Poland, South Africa, and Yugoslavia."

"The war involved the mobilization of over 100 million military personnel, making it the most widespread war in history. Over seventy million people, the majority of them civilians, were killed, making it the deadliest conflict in human history." "WWII." World War 2 History. Web. 27 Apr. 2010.

[23] **"Final solution"** "The Nazis frequently used euphemistic language to disguise the true nature of their crimes. They used the term 'Final Solution' to refer to their plan to annihilate the Jewish people. It is not known when the leaders of Nazi Germany definitively decided to implement the 'Final Solution,' [but Saul Friedlander, in *Years of Extermination, 1939-1945*, writes that Hitler's rhetoric about the 'extermination' of the Jews increased significantly between March and December 1931]. The genocide or mass destruction of the Jews was the culmination of a decade of increasingly severe discriminatory measures.

In its entirety, the 'Final Solution' called for the murder of all European Jews by gassing, shooting, and other means. Approximately six million Jewish men, women, and children were killed during the Holocaust—two-thirds of the Jews living in Europe before World War II." "Final Solution." USHMM. Web 27 Apr. 2010.

[24] **Mátészalka Ghetto** "in the northeastern parts of Trianon Hungary [established in 1918, after WWI, by the Treaty of Trianon at the Grand Trianon Palace in Versailles], the most important ghettos and entrainment centers were those of Nyiregyhasa, Mátészalka, and Kisvarda. In Mátészalka the ghetto, set within the Jewish quarter, held approximately 18,000 Jews, including close to 2000 local Jews. The remainder was brought in from neighboring communities . . . . The first transport left Mátészalka on May 19, 1943." —From Braham, Randolph L. *The Politics of Genocide: The Holocaust in Hungary*. Detroit: Wayne State UP, 2000. 121.

[25] **Auschwitz** the largest concentration camp complex of its kind established by the Nazi regime. "It included three main camps, all of which deployed incarcerated prisoners at forced labor. One of them also functioned for an extended period as a killing center. The camps were located approximately 37 miles west of Krakow, near the prewar German-Polish border in Upper Silesia, an area that Nazi Germany annexed in 1939 after invading and conquering Poland. The SS authorities established three main camps near the Polish city of Oswiecim: Auschwitz I in May 1940; Auschwitz II (also called Auschwitz-Birkenau) in early 1942; and Auschwitz III (also called Auschwitz-Monowitz) in October 1942. . . . .

At least 960,000 Jews were killed in Auschwitz. Other victims included approximately 74,000 Poles, 21,000 Roma (Gypsies), and 15,000 Soviet prisoners of war; and 10,000-15,000 members of other nationalities (Soviet civilians, Czechs, Yugoslavs, French, Germans, and Austrians).

THE LIBERATION OF AUSCHWITZ

In mid-January 1945, as Soviet forces approached the Auschwitz concentration camp complex, the SS began evacuating Auschwitz and its subcamps. SS units forced nearly 60,000 prisoners to march west from the Auschwitz camp system. Thousands had been killed in the camps in the days before these death marches began. Tens of thousands of prisoners, mostly Jews, were forced to march either northwest for 55 kilometers (approximately 30 miles) to Gliwice (Gleiwitz), joined by prisoners from subcamps in East Upper Silesia, such as Bismarckhuette, Althammer, and Hindenburg, or due west for 63 kilometers (approximately 35 miles) to Wodzislaw (Loslau) in the western part of Upper Silesia, joined by inmates from the subcamps to the south of Auschwitz, such as Jawischowitz, Tschechowitz, and Golleschau. SS guards shot anyone who fell behind or could not continue. Prisoners also suffered from the cold weather, starvation, and exposure on these marches. At least 3,000 prisoners died on route to Gliwice alone; possibly as many as 15,000 prisoners died during the evacuation marches from Auschwitz and the subcamps.

Upon arrival in Gliwice and Wodzislaw, the prisoners were put on unheated freight trains and transported to concentration camps in Germany, particularly to Flossenbürg, Sachsenhausen, Gross-Rosen, Buchenwald, Dachau, and also to Mauthausen in Austria. The rail journey lasted for days. Without food, water, shelter, or blankets, many prisoners did not survive the transport. . . .

On January 27, 1945, the Soviet army entered Auschwitz, Birkenau, and Monowitz and liberated around 7,000 prisoners, most of whom were ill and dying. It is estimated that the SS and police deported at a minimum 1.3 million people to Auschwitz complex between 1940 and 1945. Of these, the camp authorities murdered 1.1 million." "Auschwitz Concentration Camp." USHMM. Web. 27 Apr. 2010.

[26] *Appell* (roll call) "a daily feature of concentration camp life. Prisoners had to stand at roll calls morning and night. The roll calls were punitive as the prisoners were pointlessly made to stand for hours outside in inclement weather. Even dead prisoners had to be turned out and counted. Selections occurred at roll calls where the weaker prisoners would be culled for death." "Appell." Holocaust Encyclopedia. Web 27 Apr. 2010.

[27] *Sonderkommando* "a special detachment, Jewish prisoners in the death camps who worked in the gas chambers and crematoria. They took the bodies from the gas chambers, retrieved any valuables the prisoner may have hidden, including gold fillings, and brought the bodies to be burned in crematoria or to pits to be buried." From Michael, Robert, and Karin Doerr. *Nazi-Deutsch/Nazi-German: An English Lexicon of the Language of the Third Reich.* Westport, CT. Greenwood P, 2002.

28 Yom Kippur (Heb., "Day of Atonement"). Annual day of fasting and atonement, occurring in the fall on Tishri 10 (just after *Rosh HaShanah*); the most solemn and important occasion of the Jewish religious year. "Yom Kippur." Jewish Virtual Library, Glossary. Web. 27 Apr. 2010.

29 Suicide on electric fences "One deterrent to suicide in slave labor section of Auschwitz, according to Levi, was that the Germans would execute one hundred inmates for one suicide on the fences. The Germans disliked turning off the electricity to remove the body because this made the camp 'less safe.'" . . . . Anissimov notes that many *Sonderkommandos* "threw themselves into the flames of the crematorium" (qtd in Lester). —From Lester, David. *Suicide and the Holocaust.* New York: Nova Science, 2005. 112.

30 Opera Singer Sara describes an opera singer at Auschwitz. One possibility is **Ottilie Metzger-Lattermann** (1878-1943)

German soprano, Ottilie Metzger-Lattermann, whose life ended tragically in Auschwitz-Birkenau Concentration Camp, was an important German singer, graduating from early Rhine-maiden roles into the major Wagnerian parts. "Ottilie Metzger-Lattermann." Historic Opera. Web. 27 Apr. 2010.

"This splendidly gifted contralto was born in Frankfurt am Main and studied in Berlin. She taught in Berlin until her Jewish faith made escape necessary; she fled to Brussels. But for Metzger and millions like her, there was to be no safe haven. She was deported to Auschwitz in late 1942, and it is assumed she endured that hell on earth till early 1943." "Ottilie Metzger-Lattermann." Cantabile Subito. Web. 27 Apr. 2010.

See *Witness: Voices of the Holocaust*, Edith P., in "What My Eyes Have Seen: The Camps," relates that when this opera singer came to Auschwitz-Birkenau, after selection, an SS made her sing: "And he made that women, middle-aged woman, get up, stark naked, and sing" (122).

See also *Music and Manipulation*, 282-3.

31 "Used up" women These women were considered disposable. "The existence of camp brothels makes clear how women were sexually humiliated and exploited as well as robbed of all self-determination. Women were forced into sex work with male prisoners in a total of ten concentration camps. The first were in Mauthausen and Gusen; further brothels were constructed in the concentration camps Auschwitz-Stammlager, Auschwitz-Monowitz, Buchenwald, Flossenbürg, Neuen-gamme, Dachau, Sachsenhausen, and Mittelbau-Dora. In SS jargon, the camp brothel was also called a 'special building,' and was later set up in less prominent places than in Mauthausen or Gusen. The SS also began attempting to hush up the existence of the facilities whenever possible."

"Sexual exploitation of persecuted and imprisoned women was a permanent feature of the Third Reich. Forced sexual contact with male prisoners and SS soldiers, forced sterilizations, forced abortions, medical experiments, rapes, shaving their hair off—the list of major physical forms of violence is long. Another long list includes forms of sexualized psychological violence, which ranged from degrading looks and insinuating slurs to being under constant threat of sexual attacks by the SS." From Halbmayr, Brigitte, co-author. Sexualisierte Gewalt. Weibliche Erfahrungen in NS-Konzentrationslagern. Vienna: Mandelbaum, 2004. Web. 27 Apr. 2010.

See also Weitzenhof, Arnold, with Maryann McLoughlin. *This I Remember*. Margate: ComteQ, 2006. 13.

[32] **POWs** "Use of forced labor in Nazi Germany during World War II occurred on a large scale. . . . . As the war progressed, the use of slave labor experienced massive growth. **Prisoners of war** and civilian 'undesirables' were brought in from occupied territories. Millions of Jews, Slavs and other conquered peoples were used as slave laborers by German corporations such as Thyssen, Krupp, IG Farben and even *Fordwerke*—a subsidiary of the Ford Motor Company. About 12 million forced laborers, most of whom were Eastern Europeans, were employed in the German war economy inside Nazi Germany throughout the war. More than 2000 German companies profited from slave labor during the Nazi era, including Deutsche Bank and Siemens." "Forced Labor." Enwikipedia. Web. 27 Apr. 2010.

"Germany and Italy detained just under 300,000 Allied POW's (the exact number cannot be ascertained). While their captivity cannot be compared to the horrors visited upon, for example, Russians, or to that visited upon their comrades by the pernicious Japanese, theirs was still an existence marked by illness, malnutrition, hunger and monotony." —From book review in *Contemporary Review*, 2007. Gilbert, Adrian. *Allied Prisoners in Europe, 1939-1945*. London: John Murray Publishers, 2006.

[33] **Krankenbau** (Prisoner's Hospital) "Prisoners came to the hospital seeking, if nothing else, a brief respite from the killing work. When prisoners were too ill or weak they made their way or were taken to the camp 'hospital.' More often then not prisoners who came to this place either died here of 'natural causes' such as exhaustion, typhus, dysentery, were given a phenol injection in the heart, or were taken to the gas chambers." "Krankenbau." Remember. Web. 27 Apr. 2010.

[34] **Death marches** Forced marches of prisoners over long distances and under intolerable conditions. The prisoners, guarded heavily, were treated brutally and many died from mistreatment or were shot. "Death Marches." Jewish Virtual Library, Glossary. Web. 27 Apr. 2010.

[35] **Typhus** "refers to a group of infectious diseases that are caused by rickettsial organisms and that result in an acute febrile illness. Only the body louse is known to spread disease.

Without treatment the disease can be fatal, particularly the epidemic form. Prompt treatment with antibiotics cures nearly every patient.

Epidemic typhus is found most frequently during times of war and privation. For example, typhus killed hundreds of thousands of prisoners in Nazi Germany concentration camps during World War II. The deteriorating quality of hygiene in camps such as Theresienstadt and Bergen-Belsen created conditions where diseases such as typhus flourished. Situations in the twenty-first century with potential for a typhus epidemic would include refugee camps during a major famine or natural disaster." "Typhus." E medicine: Medscape. Web. 27 Apr. 2010.

[36] **UNRRA** (United Nations Relief and Rehabilitation) created at a 44-nation conference at the White House on November 9, 1943. Its mission was to provide economic assistance to European nations after World War II and to repatriate and assist the refugees who would come under Allied control. The U.S. government funded close to half of UNRRA's budget.

UNRRA assisted in the repatriation of millions of refugees in 1945 and managed hundreds of displaced persons camps in Germany, Italy, and Austria during that year. It provided health and welfare assistance to the DPs, as well as vocational training and entertainment. It administered the work of 23 separate voluntary welfare agencies, including the Joint Distribution Committee, the Organization for Rehabilitation through Training (ORT), and the Hebrew Immigrant Aid Society (HIAS). In late 1945, as the displaced persons camps were given greater autonomy, the voluntary agencies increasingly operated independently. UNRRA continued to serve as a major employer of displaced persons.

The massive and protracted relief efforts caused the agency to run out of funds and in 1947 its tasks were taken over by a successor organization, the International Refugee Organization (IRO). The new agency inherited the care of 643,000 displaced persons in 1948." "UNRRA." USHMM. Web. 27 Apr. 2010.

[37] **Joint** "Joint Distribution Committee (JDC) Since 1914, the American Jewish Joint Distribution Committee (JDC) has given global expression to the principle that all Jews are responsible for one another. Working today in over 70 countries, JDC acts on behalf of North America's Jewish communities and others to rescue Jews in danger, provide relief to those in distress, revitalize overseas Jewish communities, and help Israel overcome the social challenges of its most vulnerable citizens. JDC also provides non-sectarian emergency relief and long-term development assistance worldwide.

After the Holocaust: Rebuilding Jewish Lives and Jewish Life

As the war in Europe drew to a close, JDC marshaled its forces to meet a crisis of staggering proportions, racing to ensure that tens of thousands of newly liberated Jews would survive to enjoy the fruits of freedom. A massive purchasing and shipping program was instituted to provide urgent necessities for these Holocaust survivors in the face of critical local shortages, with 227 million pounds of supplies shipped to Europe from U.S. ports.

By late 1945, some 75,000 Jewish survivors of the Nazi horrors had crowded into the displaced-persons (DP) camps that were hastily set up in Germany, Austria, and Italy. Conditions were abominable, with many subjected to anti-Semitism and hostile treatment. Earl Harrison, dean of the University of Pennsylvania Law School, asked Joseph Schwartz, JDC's European director, to accompany him on his official tour of the camps. His landmark report called for separate Jewish camps and for UNRRA

(United Nations Relief and Rehabilitation Administration) participation in administering them—with JDC's help." "Joint." Joint Distribution Committee. Web. 27 Apr. 2010.

[38] **International Committee of the Red Cross/ Red Crescent** Growing from one man's spontaneous gesture to help wounded soldiers [Henry Dunant, founder of the International Red Cross Movement. Clara Barton, founder of the American Red Cross during the Civil War], to become an organization reaching out to millions of war victims around the world, the ICRC has worked in most of the major crises of the past 140 years. The ICRC is an independent, neutral organization ensuring humanitarian protection and assistance for victims of war and armed violence. . . . .

The ICRC is at the origin of both the International Red Cross / Red Crescent Movement and of international humanitarian law, notably the Geneva Conventions.

Under Hitler's regime, Jews were deprived of all their rights and dispossessed of their property, packed into overcrowded ghettos, forced to wear a yellow star and subjected to countless forms of humiliation and brutality, to deportation and massacres. In December 1939, the President of the International Committee of the Red Cross (ICRC) approached the German Red Cross to arrange for ICRC delegates to visit the Jews from Vienna who had been deported to Poland. He met with a refusal, as the German authorities did not under any circumstances want to enter into a discussion on the fate of these people.

From then on, the ICRC opted for a strategy of no longer addressing the question of Jews directly—it did so only in general approaches concerning the victims of mass arrests or deportation, and then it made no reference to their religious affiliation or racial origins, although it was clear that the people in question were, for the most part, Jews.

On 29 April 1942, the German Red Cross informed the ICRC that it would not communicate any information on 'non-Aryan' detainees, and asked it to refrain from asking questions about them.

Apart from the work of Friedrich Born in Hungary and a few sporadic instances elsewhere, the ICRC's efforts to assist Jews and other groups of civilians persecuted during the Second World War were a failure." "ICRC during the Holocaust." International Committee of the Red Cross/ Red Crescent. Web. 27 Apr. 2010.

See Favez, Jean-Claude. *The Red Cross and the Holocaust.* Cambridge: Cambridge UP, 1999.

[39] **Kibbutz** (Hebrew word for "communal settlement") "a unique rural community; a society dedicated to mutual aid and social justice; a socioeconomic system based on the principle of joint ownership of property, equality and cooperation of production, consumption and education; the fulfillment of the idea 'from each according to his ability, to each according to his needs'; a home for those who have chosen it." "Kibbutz." Jewish Virtual Library, Glossary. Web. 27 Apr. 2010.

[40] **Orphaned Jewish children** "After the surrender of Nazi Germany, ending World War II, refugees and displaced persons searched throughout Europe for missing children. Thousands of orphaned children were in displaced persons camps. Many surviving Jewish children fled Eastern Europe as part of the mass exodus (*Brichah*) to the western zones of occupied Germany, en route to the *Yishuv* (the Jewish settlement in Palestine). Through *Youth Aliyah* (Youth Immigration), thousands migrated to the *Yishuv*, and then to the state of Israel after its establishment in 1948." "Children during the Holocaust." USHMM. Web. 27 Apr. 2010.

[41] **Captain of the ship** "Even though it is believed to be a regular event, a ship's captain generally doesn't have the legal right to perform a wedding at sea. In order for a captain of a ship to perform a marriage at sea, he must be a judge, a justice of the peace, a minister or an officially recognize official such as a Notary Public." "How to Get Married at Sea." Marriage.about. Web. 27 Apr. 2010.

[42] **Tuberculosis** "One of the many horrible things in the camps during Nazi rule was disease. Some diseases that were present in the camps were as follows: Typhus, Typhoid, Dysentery, and Tuberculosis. The massive amount of disease was due to poor conditions in the camps. As there were no working sewer systems, excrement was every where. The people in the camp were not able to clean themselves readily, as there were few showers available, and they did not have a change of clothes. Also disease ran rampant because there were few, if any cures for them, and they had very few doctors in the camps. The doctors that were in the camps were most likely prisoners who had no medicine or instruments.

"Tuberculosis is a disease caused by the bacteria called, Mycobacterium tuberculosis. People can become infected with tuberculosis, by inhaling some of the bacteria. It can get into the air in many ways such as people who already have the disease, coughs, sneezes, shouts, or spits. However, it can not travel though touch, such as shaking hands or touching clothes. The spreading of the bacteria in the lungs can cause pneumonia. Certain lymph nodes may also be enlarged. Some symptoms of tuberculosis are weakness or tiredness, weight loss, fever, night sweats, coughing, chest pain, and shortness of breath. The body can recover from tuberculosis, or the tuberculosis can lie dormant for a period of time, which can become active." "Diseases during the Holocaust." Socyberty: Disease during the Holocaust. Web. 27 Apr. 2010.

[43] **Carlo Forlanini** (1847-1918) an Italian physician. "In 1870 he earned his medical degree from the University of Pavia, and afterwards joined the staff of the *Ospedale Maggiore* in Milan. Later he was an instructor at the Universities of Turin (1884) and Pavia (1899). In 1900 he became a professor of clinical medicine in Pavia. Today the 'Carlo Forlanini Institute' in Rome is named in his honor. He was the older brother of aviation pioneer Enrico Forlanini (1848-1930).

Carlo Forlanini was a specialist regarding tuberculosis and respiratory disorders. "Carlo Forlanini." Enwikipedia. Web. 27 Apr. 2010.

44 Merano "The history of the Jewish Community of Merano, South Tyrol, Italy, dates back to the first half of the eighteenth century. The Jews of Merano used a donation from a German family named Königswarter to establish a sanatorium for poor Jews suffering from tuberculosis (1873), two cemeteries in Bolzano and Merano, and this synagogue (1901), which is still in use. The synagogue of Innsbruck, in northern Tyrol, was built one year later.

"In the 30 years between the end of World War I and the beginning of World War II, the Jewish community grew to more than 600. A number of kosher hotels and sanatoriums were established, which became famous throughout Europe.

"Jews came to Merano from around the world. This is evident from the more than 100 places of origin referenced in the cemetery. The sanatorium treated many Jews suffering from tuberculosis, including many famous authors and scientists." "Merano." Jewish Virtual Library. Web. 27 Apr. 2010.

45 Zionism and Aliyah (Translated: ascent) *Aliyah* refers to Jewish immigration to the Land of Israel (and since its establishment in 1948, the State of Israel). The opposite action, Jewish emigration from Israel, is referred to as *Yerida* (descent). Aliyah is widely regarded as an important Jewish cultural concept and a fundamental concept of Zionism.

Zionism is the national revival movement of the Jewish people. It holds that the Jews have the right to self-determination in their own national home, and the right to develop their national culture. Historically, Zionism strove to create a legally recognized national home for the Jews in their historical homeland. This goal was implemented by the creation of the State of Israel. Today, Zionism supports the existence of the state of Israel and helps to inspire a revival of Jewish national life, culture and language. "Aliyah and Zionism." Zionism-Israel. Web. 27 Apr. 2010.

46 Haifa the largest city in Northern Israel, and the third-largest city in the country, with a population of over 265,000. Haifa has a mixed population of Jews and Arabs. It is also home to the Bahá'í World Centre, a UNESCO World Heritage Site.

Haifa, built on the slopes of Mount Carmel, has a history dating back to Biblical times. The phrase 'Haifa works, Jerusalem prays, and Tel Aviv plays' refers to Haifa's reputation as a city of workers. At the beginning of the 20th century, Haifa emerged as an industrial port city and growing population center. The British withdrew from Haifa on April 21, 1948. The city was captured on April 23, 1948 in Operation Bi'ur Hametz, by the Carmeli Brigade of the Haganah commanded by Moshe Carmel. The conflict led to a massive displacement of Haifa's Arab population.

Following the 1948 Arab-Israeli War, the city played an important role as the gateway for Jewish immigration." "Haifa." Enwikipedia. Web. 27 Apr. 2010.

[47] **Israel, nationhood** On May 14, 1948, on the day in which the British Mandate over a Palestine expired, the Jewish People's Council gathered at the Tel Aviv Museum, and approved the following proclamation, declaring the establishment of the State of Israel. The new state was recognized that night by the United States and three days later by the USSR." "Israel." Israel Ministry of Foreign Affairs. Web. 27 Apr. 2010.

[48] **Antisemitism** Prejudice against or hatred of Jews—known as antisemitism—has plagued the world for more than 2,000 years.

During the Holocaust, anti-Semitism was a factor that limited American Jewish action during the war, and put American Jews in a difficult position.

Another type of anti-Semitism in America during this time was 'passive anti-Semitism.' While many Americans would not physically harm a Jew, they had negative internal feelings towards them. Throughout history, Jews have been continuously looked down upon, and have been used as scapegoats. Therefore, during the Holocaust, 'passive anti-Semitism' meant that these people were already inclined not to care about the Jews in Europe, let alone America's response to this crisis.

There was an antisemitic feeling in Congress, as well as in the US Armed Forces. In Congress, antisemitism was a factor explaining the common hostility towards refugee immigration. Antisemitism explained Congress' actions that blocked all likely havens of refuge for the Jews.' . . . . In the military, many high up officers used words such as 'kikes,' and openly joked about antisemitic stereotypes. Furthermore, Jewish officers expressed frustration over the antisemitic attitudes in the upper ranks.

Antisemitism in the United States was also proven in national public opinion polls taken from the mid 1930s to the late 1940s. The results showed that over half the American population saw Jews as greedy and dishonest. This is a frightening proportion. These polls also found that many Americans believed that Jews were too powerful in the United States. In conclusion, anti-Semitism was seriously widespread in the U.S, in turn preventing Americans from wanting to help the Jews in Europe.

If the American public and even worse, its government, looked down upon the Jews within their own country, why would they care about aiding Jews in Europe? "American Antisemitism during the Holocaust." History, University of California, Santa Barbara. Web. 27 Apr. 2010.

"Antisemitism is a barometer for the general health of a society—when hatred of Jews flourishes, other human rights are in danger. In 2009, there are signs of increasing antisemitism across the world, including hate speech, violence targeting Jews and Jewish institutions, and denial of the Holocaust. Militant Islamic groups with political power use language suggestive of genocide regarding the State of Israel. The president of Iran declared the Holocaust a 'myth' and said Israel should be 'wiped off the map.' *Hamas*, a Palestinian terrorist organization, pledges in its founding covenant to 'obliterate' Israel.

In the aftermath of the moral failures that made the Holocaust possible, we must remain alert to antisemitism, hatred, and all forms of bigotry." "Antisemitism." USHMM. Web. 27 Apr. 2010.

In *Antisemitism in America* (Oxford UP, 1995), "Leonard Dinnerstein argues that deeply ingrained hostility toward Jews embedded in Christian teachings is the mainspring of this prejudice. During the Civil War, he notes, Jews became scapegoats for the ills of society; non-Jews in both the North and South accused Jews of profiteering and of supporting the enemy. Pivotal historical periods such as the Great Depression years and life on the home front during World War II are also fully explored. This scapegoating continued, Dinnerstein shows, through the Great Depression and into WW II, when Charles Lindbergh, addressing an isolationist rally in Iowa in 1941, blamed Jews for pushing the U.S. toward war with Germany. Professor of History at the University of Arizona, Dinnerstein offers an illuminating analysis of black antisemitism since WW II, tracing its roots in many instances to Protestant theology. Noting that antagonism toward Jews has always been weaker in the U.S. than in Europe, he predicts that countervailing traditions of tolerance, legal equality and pluralism will continue to weaken antisemitism in America." —From *Publishers Weekly* 1995 review.

[49] *Caipirinha* Brazil's national cocktail, made with cachaça, sugar, and lime. Like rum, Cachaça is made from sugarcane alcohol, obtained from the fermentation of sugarcane juice that is afterwards distilled. The word *caipirinha* is the diminutive version of the word *caipira*, which refers to someone from the countryside. "*Caipirinha.*" Enwikipedia. Web. 27 Apr. 2010.

[50] **Masada** (Hebrew, pronounced *Metzada*, from *metzuda*, fortress) "the name for a site of ancient palaces and fortifications in the South District of Israel on top of an isolated rock plateau, or large mesa, on the eastern edge of the Judean Desert overlooking the Dead Sea. After the First Jewish-Roman War (also known as the Great Jewish Revolt) a siege of the fortress in 70 CE by troops of the Roman Empire led to the mass suicide of 960 Jewish rebels, who preferred death to surrender.

"Masada today is one of the Jewish people's greatest symbols. Israeli soldiers take an oath there: "Masada shall not fall again." Next to Jerusalem, Masada is the most popular destination of Jewish tourists visiting Israel." "Masada." Jewish Virtual Library. Web. 27 Apr. 2010.

Discussion Questions

Pre-reading Classroom Activities:

1. Look up "Czechoslovakia" in the *Holocaust Encyclopedia* online at the ushmm.org website, under additional resources A-Z. Read the article, noting the dates and people involved.

2. Look at the maps at the beginning of the book. See the first map. What country? Then look at the rest of maps to see how many countries the Pauls live in before they settle in the U.S.

Reading Activities:

1. List the people who are mentioned in the memoir. Can you describe them?

2. How is the book organized? Explain.

3. Why was the book titled *Sara Triumphant?* Explain.

4. Why did the Pauls leave Israel? Research conditions in Israel in 1947 to 1950.

5. Make a timeline from the beginning of Sara's life to the end. Include the important events in Sara's life

6. Discuss the significance of family to Sara.

7. Discuss the significance of religion to Sara?

8. Symbols are objects that stand for or represent something else. Explain the symbolism (what they represent or stand for) of Sara's earrings, of her grandmother's apron pockets, of the electrified fence at Auschwitz-Birkenau, of the sea in Italy, of Moria Resort, of Masada, and Passover.

9. Write about a holiday during which you spent time with family members.

10. Describe two of the photographs. Do you have photographs similar (not the same) to these in your family album?

Post-reading Classroom Activities:

1. Using the chart below, prepare an identity chart for yourself. Consider all the factors—family, school, hobbies, nationality, ethnicity, religion, etc.—that influence how you think about yourself and make decisions.

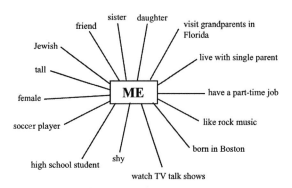

Sample Chart

2. Prepare identity charts for Sara Paul. Make sure to include influences before, during, and after World War II and the Holocaust (Shoah).

3. Write a letter to the Ernest Paul, Sra's husband, commenting on the book and/or asking him questions.

4. Write a letter to Ernest Paul, Sara's husband, asking him to come speak with your class. Prepare three questions that you would ask him.

5. Have a "Sara Paul Day" in your school. Teach the other classes at your grade level about Sara Paul, her experiences during the Shoah, and immigration to Israel and the U.S. Make posters and/or power points to educate the other grades. Invite Ernest Paul, Sara's husband, to an assembly for all the students in your grade.

<u>For Further Reflection</u>:

1. According to the scholar Samantha Power, an ***upstander*** is an individual who takes risks to help others in danger and does not hesitate to criticize those who fail to help others in need or danger. Describe the upstanders in *Sara Triumphant!* Do you know any upstanders?

2. Think about historical events that have intersected with and influenced your life. Discuss these.

3. Discuss how silence and indifference to the human and civil rights of the Jews helped the perpetrators.

4. What are the obligations of responsible citizens in a democratic society?